Africa Give Me Your Eyes

Stories about meeting people in Kenya

Mathew Haumann MHM

translated by R. van Eyndhoven

Source Books   Trabuco Canyon   California

Text copyright © Matthew Haumann MHM
Illustrations © Janet Mullen
Cover Painting by Mathew Haumann
Typsetting & Design by Studio 185
Translation by R. van Eyndhoven

Much of this book was originally published by Stichting Gezamenlijke Missiepubliciteit, Deurne, Holland, under the title *Achter De Bloemen Van Nairobi*. This edition first published: 1997.

Properly attributed quotations and copies of up to 100 words of continuous text may be used without prior permission. For use of longer passages, please enquire of the publisher.

Library of Congress Cataloging–in–Publication Data

Haumann, Mathew.
    [Achter de bloemen van Nairobi. English]
    Africa give me your eyes : stories about meeting people in Kenya / Mathew Haumann.
    p. cm.
    ISBN 0-940147-44-0
    1. Kenya--Social life and customs. 2. Missions--Kenya.
3. Haumann, Mathew. I. Title.
DT433.54.H38   1997
967.62--dc21   97-1570
                                                                              CIP

ISBN 0-940147-44-0

Published by:

Source Books
P.O. Box 794
Trabuco Canyon CA 92678

Printed and bound in the USA by KNI Inc., Anaheim CA

You want to see with my eyes.
Give me your heart,
and I'll give you my eyes.
—A͏FRICAN S͏AGE

To all who are willing to listen
to Africa with their hearts.

CONTENTS

To Sit Where the People Sit	1
Nairobi	5
Kamau Mfupi	9
A Sunday Morning	13
The Poor Don't Get Tired	19
Hassan	25
Charlie	29
The Freedom Fighter	35
A Light in the Darkness	39
The Sewing Group	43
Pagan Justice	48
The Witch Doctor	52
Son Kasuki	57
Undugu Beat	61
Grace	65
Parkingboy	71
God Will Look After Everything	76
Attempted Murder	81
Helping Others to Help Themselves	84
Your Own Child	89
Musinya	93
Kirimi	97
In the Monastery	100
Nimeshindwa	105
Matatu	110
Dead and Buried	113
A Coat Full of Lice	117
Crime	122
A Fairytale Wedding	126
Fullblood	131
Notes	134

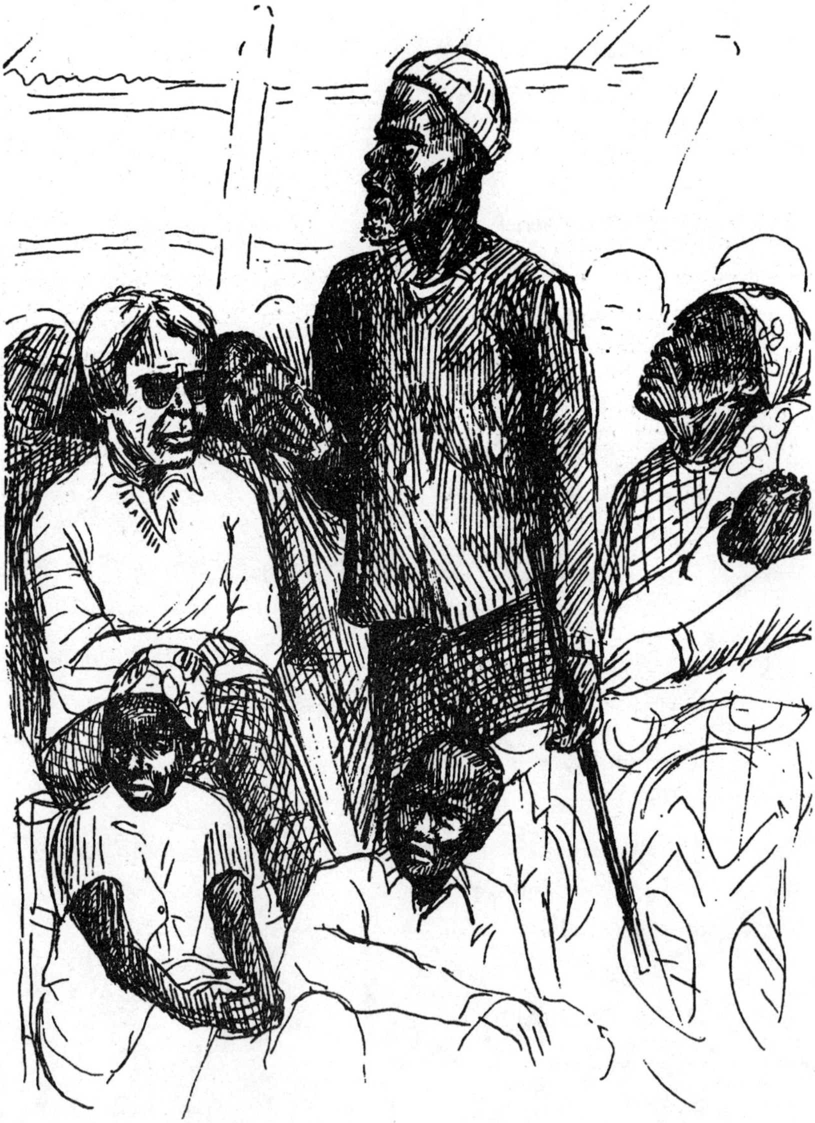

Talking to each other is loving each other. —Kikuyu saying

TO SIT WHERE THE PEOPLE SIT

Sitting under a tree chatting with the natives is not the typical picture we have of a missionary. For the most part, writers of African mission history have concerned themselves with the enormous achievements in education, health care and the establishment and expansion of the local church. Far be it from me to detract from these achievements. Often missionaries were a breed apart: hardened men and women who took the initiative, not bowing to difficulties. They were realistic and pragmatic. Asking the Africans for advice and listening to it was often considered a time-wasting luxury. Or perhaps we did not listen to the Africans because we thought they had nothing to tell us. Or could it be, that we missionaries clung to our own certainties? Though he gave Christianity a warm welcome, the African too, often stuck to his own traditional certainties. People don't trust what they don't know. In this, both the African and the Western missionary are cut from the same cloth.

But how could I have the temerity to presume that the African listening to me should change his or her life and way of thinking, if as a missionary, I were not willing to return the compliment? There is no doubt that Mission can be considered a dialogue between different religions, different cultures. It is a meeting of people. And the missionary risks his or her own beliefs and certainties in the transaction. If the risk is not run the riches of Africa and the Africans remain hidden.

Often our starting point as missionaries, was our claim to the monopoly on eternal truth. It did not cross our minds that in other ways of thinking we might discover new truths. Christianity has been deeply influenced by Jewish, Greek and Roman modes of thought. But perhaps we shall have a better understanding of Christ, if we see Him not only with the eyes of the Jews, Greeks or Romans, but also with the eyes of all cultures of the world, including those of Africa.

There is a dialogue with the East. Christianity's relationship with the East is not one-sided. The Church listens to the mysticism, the spirituality of India and Japan. Zen masters teach us to meditate, and Oriental spirituality enriches the Church. In like manner, liberation theology, with its genesis in South America, is a source of inspiration for many of us. But the dialogue with Africa has hardly begun. Our relationship with Africa and the Africans involves the history of prejudice and mistrust. We are the poorer for that, and it is one of the reasons why conflicts with Africa continue.

Laurens van der Post, who grew up with Africans and was partly raised by an African nanny often wrote about those African riches. In one of his books he says,

> There is no solution for the conflict in Africa, or in the world, unless there is first of all a change in the heart and understanding of man, and I do not see how that change of heart can come about until the white man in Africa starts to think about himself in a new way... We force the African continually to take from us and prevent him from giving to us in his own rich way; we deny Africa its own unique creativeness. [†]

Laurens van der Post was not writing about missionaries, but I believe that his words hold good for the missionary. Our mission is not only about the conversion of Africa, but also about the conversion, the complete change, of ourselves.

Fortunately, during my stay in Africa there have been many times when a true dialogue with Africans has come about. Often they were during periods when I felt defeated, or when I was willing to let myself be led rather than lead. These times have been very potent. They set me free from the heavy baggage I brought to Africa. Such dialogue hardly can be organized; it just happens at those times when people are together in willing, mutual receptivity.

[†] Laurens van der Post, *The Dark Eye in Africa,* Morrow & Co., New York, 1955

I have written of some of these encounters because I think they can enrich others just as they have enriched me.

Sitting under a tree chatting with the natives is often considered by Westerners to be a waste of time. Africans call it *making time*. Making time might be called an African cottage industry. In our culture there are very few people left who know how to make time. The Africans often make time under the tree, for themselves, for each other, but also for the missionary, if he is willing to accept it. I spent over thirty years in Africa: in Kenya, Sudan and Zaïre. Often I spent my time being busy—running around. But luckily there were always moments when the Africans slowed me down, where they invited me to sit with them under the tree. There under the tree, the dialogue about what really constitutes Mission is born.

I am still looking for a good definition of Mission. One that appeals to me more and more is: *Mission is to sit where the people sit and let God happen.*

CENTRAL AND EASTERN NAIROBI

When you are rich, you are hated,
When you are poor, you are despised. —Ashanti proverb

NAIROBI

> Nairobi, a bleak, swampy stretch of soppy landscape, windswept, devoid of human habitation of any sort, the resort of thousands of wild animals of every species. The only evidence of occasional presence of human kind is the old caravan track skirting the bog-like plain.

In these words R. O. Preston described Nairobi in 1899.

There *was* a human presence, of course. The Maasai, a nomadic tribe of the Rift Valley, came here regularly to herd their cows, sheep and goats. But they did not leave behind as many tell-tale signs of their presence as Westerners do. Or, it may be the case that colonials such as Preston considered the Maasai other than human. These are the people who gave this place a name. They called it *Enkare Nairobi,* which means 'The Place of Cool Water.' They were proud herdsmen, with a reputation for great courage, protecting their herds with spears against attacks from wild animals. Many of them are still in Nairobi, no longer as proud herdsmen, but fearless nonetheless. They are employed as night watchmen, protecting the sleeping rich against robbers.

> Nairobi is a beautiful city with many open spaces, parks and gardens surrounding its mini skyscrapers and odd reminders of its birth as a railway town, a little more than seventy years ago. The main streets are a riot of colour with bougainvilleas, hibiscus, oleanders and the glorious blue flowering jacaranda trees. Nairobi is often called 'the safari capital of the world.'

This is written on the tourist map of Kenya for 1981. Such a description belongs on a tourist map. Although it is not untrue, it is not the whole truth. Another name for Nairobi in the tourist brochures is *City in the Sun.* That too is true for much of the year, but in the musical, *Portraits of Survival,* the parkingboys and the prostitutes sing *Where is the sun for us?* They, and many others, have the right to ask the question, as Nairobi is clearly a two-faced city. It has the face of the tourist and conference city, full of luxury and comfort. It is the heart of the government, the centre of the national and international elite which comes along with the powerful multinationals. Ambassadors live here in beautiful villas and palaces with extravagant gardens. The swimming pools of the rich are never without water, and the golf courses are of international standard.

As to the other face: most of the more than one million inhabitants live in the city's backyard, in the greatest poverty, and the number is growing. They helped to build the city in the sun, and they sweep the streets in the wealthy areas, whilst in their own back alleys the garbage is rarely collected. Now and again the tourist might meet these people in the parkingboy, the prostitute, or the driver of the VW combi in which he goes on safari.

The people live in the slums of Mathare Valley, New Grogan Road, Pumwani, Kitui, Kinyago, just to mention a few in East Nairobi. There are many other slums, some of the names you will not find on a map, for officially they do not exist. On the map they are vague white tracts. But do not think that I have invented them. Mathare Valley was put on the map as an inhabited area only after a cholera epidemic broke out some years ago, and its substantial population could be denied no longer. These precincts are not mentioned in the tourist brochures, nor should they be. Poverty is not something for rubbernecking, for photo-souvenirs. These are not areas for sightseeing.

There is no space here. There are no beautiful flowers or trees. Every square meter is packed with people. The Nairobi and Mathare Rivers no longer remind anyone of cool waters. They have become stinking open sewers. Often these parts are called the 'self-help city,' as nearly everything here has been created by the people themselves out of what is discarded by the rich city.

The contrast between wealth and poverty in Nairobi is sharp. In the rich quarters fewer than five hundred people live in a square kilometre. In Mathare Valley nearly fifty thousand are packed into such a space. The house rents in the 'good' areas of Nairobi are often more per month than a poor person earns in a year. Yet the rich can pay this without any difficulty, or it is paid for them by the company, the government, or the boss back in Europe or North America. More often than not, the poor man cannot afford the thousand shillings for his hovel in Mathare Valley or a room in Eastleigh. It is far more than a half month's salary for him. He moves to places like New Grogan or Kinyago to build his own dwelling: a hut of throwaway polythene and cardboard.

Relations between the different tribes of old in Kenya are not very good. They nickname one another, usually in an uncomplimentary manner. Here in Nairobi, two new tribes are being formed, the tribe of the rich and the tribe of the poor. The rich talk about the poor with a certain contempt, or perhaps a little fear. They call them the *Watu,* the simple folk, with the colonial connotation of 'good-for-nothings.' The poor call the rich, with a mixture of contempt and jealousy, the *Wabenzi,* which means 'those Mercedes Benz people.' Another name for them is the *Wamba kali,* which means 'dangerous dogs,' for outside the gates of nearly all the houses of the rich you will see a board on which is written, 'Beware of the Dog.'

From 1978 till 1986, with a few colleagues, I worked in some of these slums. When I say 'worked' it doesn't mean we achieved a lot. Even when we did undertake quite a bit, we didn't make a great contribution to the solution of the enormous problems here. Perhaps we even created a few new ones.

When I arrived in Kenya in 1963, things seemed simpler and I felt more confident. These days we don't have all the answers. Often we don't even have the right questions. Together with the people we have to search every day anew for what it means to be a Christian in such situations.

Poverty means great injustice. Still, poor people often are rich in spirit, with a strong urge to survive. My best moments here are when I just sit and listen. The people are worthwhile listening to.

Maybe that 'work' of ours mainly consists in letting the people know they are worthwhile, when society tells them they are not. This is bringing 'good news.' But the people have much to give to us too. In these stories I want to share some of that with you.

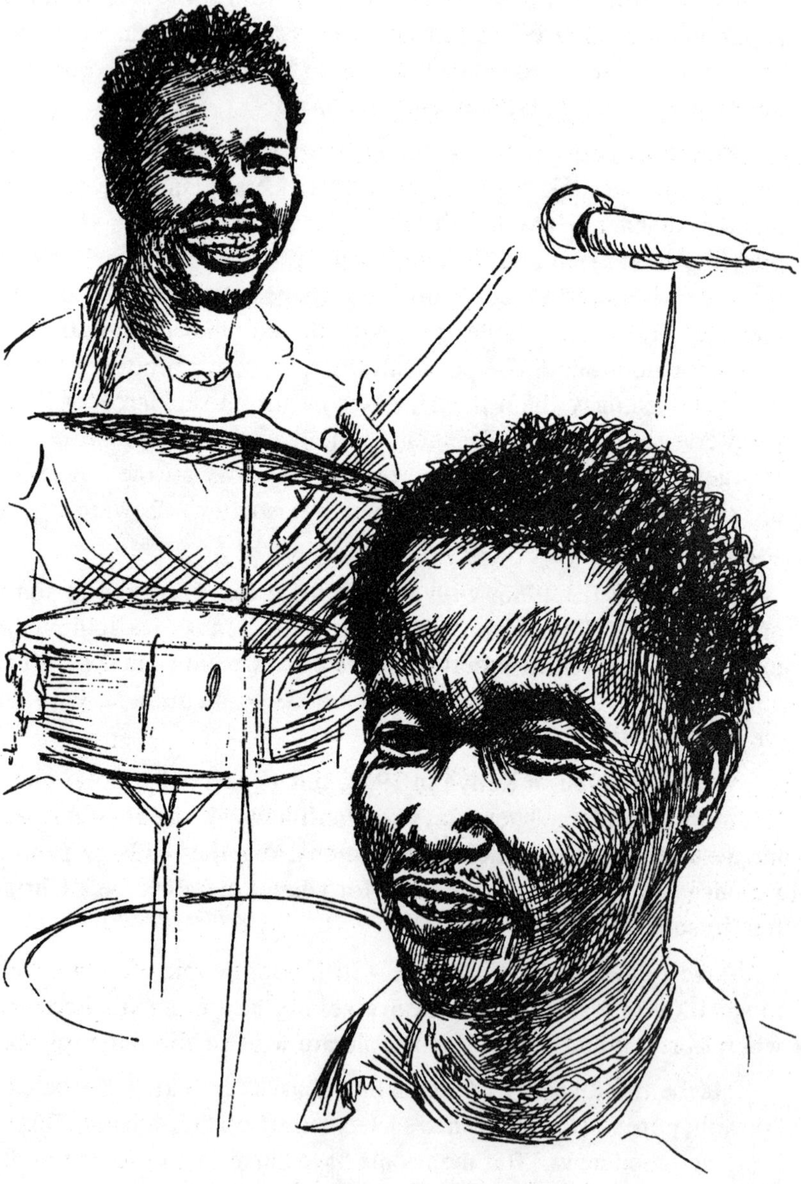

The man who warms himself at the fire while the sun is shining, does so for a reason. —KIKUYU PROVERB

KAMAU MFUPI

Kamau Mfupi is full of beans again. His old face assumes the aspect of a child as he beats the drums for the Undugu[1] traditional dancers. You can see he enjoys the rhythm of the dance, the rhythm he sets, leading the dancers with his drum. He sparks to life as he bashes away. It hasn't always been like this: Kamau Mfupi's tale is a troubled one.

In English we would call him Shorty Smith, for Kamau is a common name in Kikuyu,[2] much as Smith in England and America. He is called Shorty not only because the other Kamau in the dance group is tall, but also because he has been short and small his whole life. A penny doesn't become a shilling, it is said. Kamau knows this to be quite true, and he also knows that a penny is only a pennyworth. For many years he had very little to spend.

Kamau was born in the 'reserve' somewhere between Thika and Nyeri, about forty miles from Nairobi. He vaguely remembers the hut of mud and grass where he was brought up, and the garden with maize and sweet potatoes. His father died before he was old enough for school. He loved his mother very much indeed, but after his father's funeral she left the home and went to Nairobi. Perhaps she did not want to be inherited, as Kikuyu custom required. Perhaps she went to look for relatives, or she may have had other reasons for going; Kamau does not know. Whatever the reason, he lost her.

His grandmother looked after him. At least she gave him something to eat and an occasional beating. But grandmothers are not mothers. Grandmothers tend to be old; they are often sick and they are always in danger of dying. They don't have school fees for you. They are superstitious and often they think they are being poisoned.

Perhaps Kaumau's grandmother really was being poisoned. In any case, she was very sick when at the age of ten Kamau went to look for his mother. A dying grandmother was too much for him to handle; his mother should come. He had heard that she was in Nairobi. He knew which road to take, but he had no idea what forty miles meant.

He went off on his little bare feet. Evening fell. He was tired, but he started running so as to be in Nairobi before dark. He wanted to be with his mother that night. In the end he slept in some brush by the road; he would reach Nairobi tomorrow.

Along the way he asked for food, but people thought that a boy should be eating at his home with his mother. Kamau wanted nothing better, and so he walked on. He does not remember how long he was on the way to Nairobi: a week, perhaps two or more. The road was interminable. He gave up asking people for things to eat, instead digging up the odd cassava root and scrumping bananas; he took food whenever he found it.

Occasionally, the scruffy boy would be beaten up and he soon learned to run for it when people shouted Thief! He tried to get a ride on a bus, but after a short distance he was kicked off because he had no fare. He tried hitchhiking, but who would stop for a dirty little boy of ten? During those long days and that great distance—the forty miles were more like four hundred to the boy— just one man stopped and gave Kamau a lift for the last few miles to the dazzling city of Nairobi.

There he stood, flabbergasted: cars raced by, throngs of people, buildings up to the sky. People would suddenly hasten across the street and then freeze at the next corner. Lights, green at one moment, and red the next. It all looked very marvelous indeed. But how would he find his mother in all this? He was quite dumbfounded.

With a hungry stomach he slept that night in a park. Only flowers grew there, nothing that you could eat. He felt more alone here than on the long road, and he was very scared.

The following day he went to look for his mother. When he began to inquire, people regarded him as another little beggar and simply laughed. It was a laughable question, of course—imagine in the middle of London or New York asking for Mrs. Smith. Sometimes grownups can be very harsh and show very little understanding.

Kamau joined a gang of street urchins, parkingboys,[3] who collected a little money by helping people to find parking places for their cars. It was a tough life; sometimes you managed to earn a little money. At other times you got your ears boxed. You had to be careful when the police were around, the best thing was to run for it—and fast. On many occasions it was more profitable to steal from a car, but it was also more risky.

This group of boys took him along to Mathare Valley. They knew that mothers of abandoned children lived there—their own mothers. The search for 'Mrs. Smith' continued. There were many women with the right name, many Mamas Kamau, but either they did not come from the right place or if they did, they claimed not to know the boy. He managed to stay alive on the streets and he remained small. This eventually led to his downfall—perhaps it was a blessing in disguise, Kamau Mfupi cannot say.

The police catch the smaller boys first, and Kamau was caught more than once. At long last he was placed in a remand home for four years by the Juvenile Court. "Even if you are stupid, even if you know nothing, like myself ," Kamau says, "they can teach you all kinds of things there."

This Shorty Smith is proud that he now knows how to read and write, and that he learned the tinsmith's trade. In the home he even got a chance to make music. It was there that he learned to play the drums. He beats the drum now, and he beams with joy as everybody dances to his rhythm. He leads the singing, and the whole dance group answers its chorus.

On top of getting an education, Kamau's fortunes took another direction. The police started looking for his mother, and in such matters the police are often more successful than small boys. Kamau thinks that this was the greatest and happiest thing of all—they found his mother for him.

Kamau has never told me about that first meeting with his mother, and I don't think I should ask. His mother lives in a small hut in Mathare Valley, just as the other boys thought she might. She keeps alive by distilling and selling chang'aa.[4] Not a very respectable profession perhaps, but she is happy to be reunited with her son. Kamau Mfupi has a mother again after all these years. She spoils him a bit now and then, and Kamau is quite happy about that. His mother has seen many men go to ruin by drinking the chang'aa she brews. She occasionally drinks it herself, but she has asked her son to stay away from the stuff. So Kamau does not drink it at home; he borrows the money from his mother to buy it elsewhere.

Kamau may be a trained tinsmith now, but he has no tools and he has no job. He just hangs around with the dance group. Many members of the dance group have histories similar to Kamau's. They dance together, and if they have the money, they drink together, too. As I said before, Kamau really enjoys his drumming and he makes this group come to life. But he won't make a living this way.

The Undugu Society has offered him a loan to buy some tools. It is about time that he started to work. At twenty he is the right age. Kamau Mfupi quite agrees; it is certainly a good idea, but he is in no great hurry. He continues to sing, beat his drum and dance with the people. Perhaps he first wants to make up for some lost childhood, a childhood in which you play, laugh and do silly things, a time when your mother spoils you a little, and who can begrudge him that? However, sometime soon I will have to go and talk to Kamau about his future, and I don't relish the prospect. Do I have the right to end his childhood before he has lived it to the full?

Not all Sundays are Sundays. —Kikuyu proverb

A SUNDAY MORNING

It is a rainy morning. There is no sun, for the sky is full of clouds. On such days people living in the slums immediately adjust their clocks, the clocks which you won't find on their walls or mantelpieces. Now everything will start later, but since I have a wristwatch, I arrive at the appointed time in the igloo village[5] near the Nairobi River. We are to celebrate the Eucharist. A few people put their heads through the small openings of their polythene huts and wave their greetings; children begin to stretch, their eyes still heavy with sleep.

A couple of transistor radios blare out the news, but for one owner it doesn't seem worth listening to, and he changes over to Congolese music. That should be enough noise to wake them up. Since we have no church bell, I have brought a megaphone with me. I give this to one of the village leaders who walks around the village calling the people to prayer.

I wait more patiently than I feel. I look around; there are over two hundred huts here, strewn about without any plan whatsoever. They are constructed of all kinds of materials, mostly the waste products of the city factories. Dwellings are made of cardboard and polythene fixed over frames of bamboo. Some are ingeniously pinned together with thorns. People are camping here, not knowing where they will eventually settle. They have been here for years, but the erection of new buildings pushes them even closer to the stinking Nairobi River. There are no latrines, and the people defecate beside the river.

There is a water tap but the supply has been cut off because the bill was not paid. Water is free only when there is an outbreak of cholera in the area. Now the people have to buy their water at a high price from the water-vendors, or they use the water from the 'sewer,' as the Nairobi River is called, and risk picking up worse diseases than cholera.

The children start arriving first. Jim, a student of theology, who accompanied me this morning, has brought his guitar. He gets the children singing as we move to the church. Following good Catholic custom the church is the largest building in the village. Architecturally, it fits in well with the environment—a few poles in the ground, walls of cardboard, and a roof made of old tins and pieces of plastic sheeting. Today it is the church—tomorrow it may be the community hall, or a classroom or meeting room for the youth club. It has been swept thoroughly, and even the goat droppings have disappeared.

Helen Njoki enters, carrying a baby under one arm, and a small table under the other. The small table will serve as an altar.

Marie Louise, who has been looking tired and worried lately, brings an embroidered cloth, our altar covering. Then she runs home; she hasn't finished doing her hair yet. Maina, who is coughing badly, comes over to me and asks for a cigarette. I don't think it will do him much good, but I give him one all the same. They don't do me any good either.

People begin to trickle in, each person carrying a small stool or an old tin to sit on. I am given a real chair. The people have arrived and the church has been furnished; we can begin.

As an entrance hymn we sing *Simama, simama imara*, expressing something similar to 'Stand firm, don't give up.' We are told, 'Be on your guard, take courage and dare to trust in God.' We have only a few hymn books as most people here can't read. Those who can't read usually know the chorus and they hum along with the rest of the hymn.

Enter Njoroge, one of the village leaders. He remains standing at the entrance, a little uncertain of what to do. He isn't a Catholic, but belongs to one of the independent churches. He is not sure whether this is an exclusively Catholic affair, so I give him the megaphone and ask him to say a word of welcome. His face beams all over and he takes off his cap, something which he probably keeps on even in bed. He gives a kind of sermon and talks about God a lot more easily than I do; he talks as if he knows Him personally, and concludes with, "There are many religions but *Mungu ni Moja* —God is one. *Mungu ni Moja* and we too have to be one; we have to be united."

We then ask forgiveness, not only from God, but also from each other. This is because we often mess things up for one another. Frequently we are not united, not one. Njoroge nods; he knows that it is true in his village.

Then we have another hymn, a guitar and a drum replacing the organ. To sing is to pray twice, they say.

Today's gospel reading: *You must not call anyone on earth 'father' since you have only one Father and He is in heaven* (Matthew 23: 8-10), sounds a bit ironic around here, where very few children know their own father. They would love to have a father right here, not only in heaven.

Instead of a monologue sermon from me, we share our feelings and thoughts about the readings. We talk about life in the slums. My questions do not remain just rhetorical, for the people answer spontaneously. When I ask which song they would like to sing next they reply, *Simama.* Jim smiles and starts to play it on his guitar. We have to use the megaphone when the noise of fighting drunks outside becomes too much. Margaret, a young girl, takes it from me as if to say, "You can't sing anyway." She leads everyone in the hymn, and, as it catches on, people begin to clap their hands. The old Kibogo, with tearful eyes, sways to and fro half in ecstasy (or has she had a drink instead of breakfast?). People leave her alone; she is one of us. We have a collection. Today it is for buying charcoal which is needed to boil milk for the children's programme. This is a programme we started a few months ago. Everyone gives what he or she can spare. Mothers give their small children five cents each which they bring forward to put in the plate. A woman comes forward with a shilling coin, and at first she wants to change

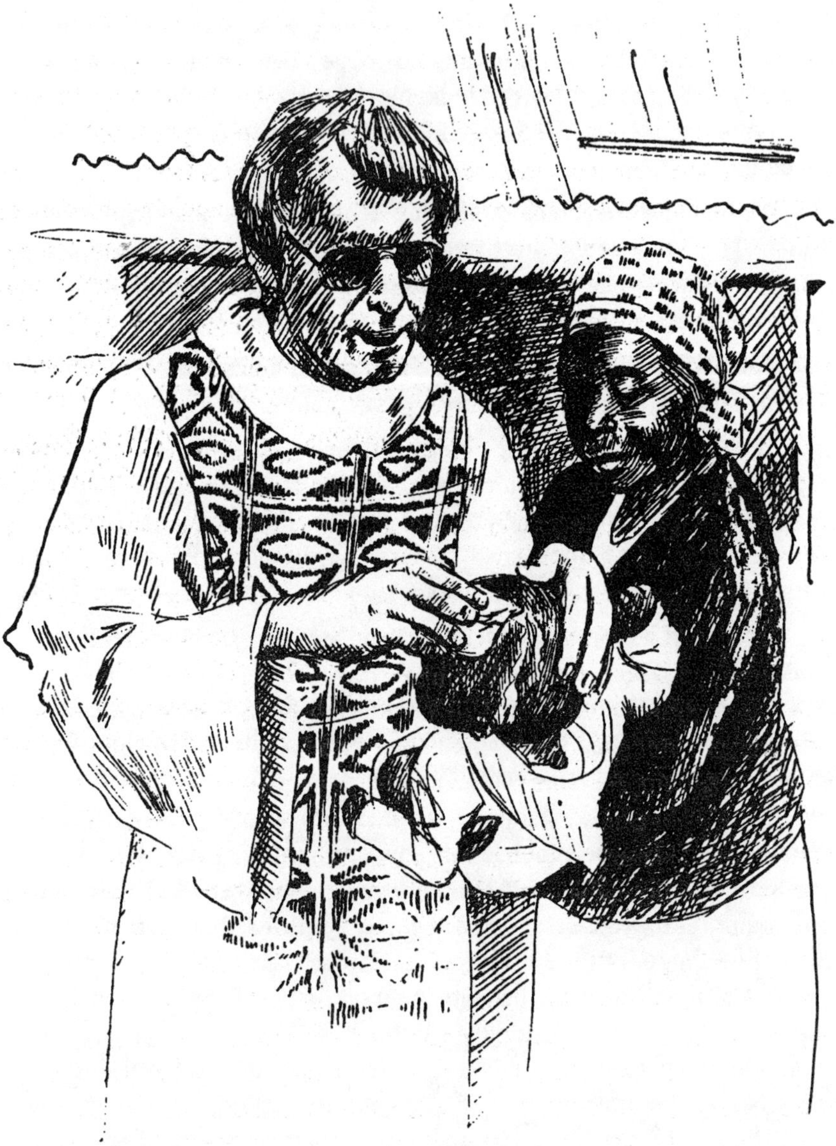

it, but then she says, "Leave it; after all, it is for our children." The collection is placed on the altar—thirty-four shillings, quite a gift for these poor people.

When we start the bidding prayers, several people stand up to say a prayer, each praying in his or her own language. This is how it should be; one ought to pray in one's own language. This is the language that God understands, and these people know it. It strikes me that non-Catholics find it easier to pray spontaneously.

I haven't the slightest idea how many of these people are Catholics. But I do know that historical and theological differences between Catholic and Protestant churches have little to do with the lives of these people in the slums. We have brought a divided Christianity to Kenya, but these people who share their lives every day are much more ecumenical than the respectable members of our official churches in Kenya and Europe.

An old woman, who has been drunk every time I have met her, starts to disturb our celebration. At first people just tell her to keep quiet, until she slips on the ground near the little table that is our altar. Only the children find this funny, and while the singing of *Holy, holy...* drowns her shouting, two men get hold of her and take her home. It is a pity that she could not stay like old Kibogo.

Before communion, we wish each other peace, even if we know that this afternoon we will quarrel again. This does not mean that we do not want peace. We shake hands with each other, some very heartily using both hands. The children especially want to shake my hand; it is something of a game for them. If I were not careful, they would push over the shaky little altar. There are not so many communicants: non-Catholics feel that they can't receive. There are all these church laws governing the sacraments which were made before we knew about the lives of people in the slums.

At the end of the celebration I bless these people as wholeheartedly as possible. "What will be the last hymn?" I ask. *Simama.* Three times the same song, but it is good like this. They sing, clap their hands, and a young girl beats the drum vigorously. An old man starts dancing; he thinks the Mass is over. I think it is still part of the Mass and I encourage him. A few women join him.

The rest stand around them swaying along and clapping their hands. When the hymn is finished they start it again. At last, they end up cheering and laughing. *Simama, simama, imara*—keep fighting for a better life, keep hoping.

> Take a stand!
> Stand firm; be on your guard!
> The word of the Lord is powerful
> Watch and pray every day
> And you will overcome (Matthew 26:41).
>
> Hills and valleys will be leveled
> The word of the Lord is powerful
> It will remain forever.
>
> We are filled with the love of God,
> The spirit of truth,
> Be the guarantee
> Of the strength we find in him (Ephesians 1).
>
> Our days of service are few
> Let's be strong, courageous
> The Spirit of Jesus stays with us
> Till the end (John 14).
>
> In all things we shall overcome
> By his power
> Who can separate us
> From his love? (Romans 8)
>
> Blessed is he who keeps the word
> Of God's Son
> Indeed, I am coming soon!
> Come, Lord Jesus!
>
> When the Lord comes to the wedding feast
> Have your lamp ready,
> Go and meet him joyfully,
> And enter, together with him (Matthew 25).

A Sunday morning service indeed, and I am glad that it still can be a celebration for these people.

Poverty is slavery. —SOMALI PROVERB

THE POOR DON'T GET TIRED

It is early for me, half past six, as I walk along Juja Road. However, it looks as if Mathare Valley is emptying. People are on their way to work or are beginning to hunt for some. They are hurrying along as if they are already late.

It is still cold. The sun has not yet poked through the clouds. People walk quickly—in groups, yet alone, hands deep in their pockets with little conversation at all. The road is full of traffic. Many people are waiting at the bus stop. When a bus arrives, the whole 'queue' surges forward. Only a few manage to squeeze themselves in, packing the bus much fuller than its makers ever could have imagined. Two or three young men cling to the outside of the bus and snatch a ride, at least until the next stop.

Matatus,[6] cheap taxi-vans bursting with people, push their way through the traffic, hooting. The boys, hanging out of the open back doors, shout their various destinations. A few more people doggedly wriggle themselves in. 'Full' matatus don't exist; there is always room for one more.

Stephen Waithaka crosses the road with his handcart full of cabbages, potatoes and bananas. He is on his way to Mathare Valley. He calls out a "Good morning" to me though he has been up for some hours already. He half hangs between the shafts of the barrow as he pulls his way through the traffic, placing a great deal of faith in the brakes of the cars pressing about him. He is nearly knocked down by a matatu, on the side of which is written, 'May God Save You.' Drivers hoot and curse, but Stephen doesn't seem at all concerned. On the side of his handcart is written, *Maskini haichoki*—The poor don't get tired. Beneath this, the owner's name is written; it is not Stephen's name.

Stephen Waithaka rents this handcart. Every morning at five o'clock he goes from Pumwani to the vegetable market, and he collects his usual load of vegetables for women in Mathare Valley. It is a heavy load, and he looks over his shoulder to see if the boy at the back is still pushing. The boy quickly starts pushing again. A taxi with the name 'Happy D Tours' blocks the way but Stephen does not move; the taxi driver will have to make a detour, happy or not.

A street preacher is holding forth at the bus stop. Nobody seems to pay much attention except the bar-girls at the bar across the street. They pause in their work of stacking the empty beer crates on the pavement, and listen for a few moments, then smile and resume.

I have already decided not to give a long sermon to the African Sisters where I am now going to say Mass; it is obviously too early for that.

A few men enter a tea kiosk called 'Cloud Nine' for a quick cup of tea and a slice of bread.

Another bus arrives, and again the crowd at the bus stop surges forward. A girl, dressed like a lady, just misses the bus. She is standing in front in her high-heeled shoes and is clutching a handbag. During the confusion of trying to get into the bus, a young lad pinches her bottom. She flares up, and loudly castigating him, tries to hit him with her handbag. He just manages to jump onto the running-board of the bus, leaving the incensed young lady behind. The men near her snigger. She goes and stands aside from them, by herself and deeply offended.

While I am celebrating the Eucharist with the Sisters, the driver of the heavy truck outside the window is trying out the engine. Heavy oil tankers and other lorries are parked at night in nearly every side street of Eastleigh. That engine sounds good and powerful to me and as far as I am concerned it can leave. But the driver remains sitting there, his foot on the accelerator, just revving up. Perhaps he is waiting for his companion before starting the long journey ahead. All these big-rigs parked here overnight are driven from Mombasa to Uganda or Burundi, and back again. The noise disturbs me, but the Maasai watchman remains unperturbed, sleeping in front of the open convent door after keeping watch all night.

After Mass the first rays of sun come through. The street is just as crowded as it was an hour ago, but now the crowds are mainly of schoolchildren. They talk, shout and run on their way to school. All are dressed smartly in uniforms, each school having a different colour and design. The boys of St. Theresa's even wear ties. This is the hour of day when even the matatus stop at the pedestrian crossings.

Stephen Waithaka is just returning with his barrow. His load is no longer heavy, only a few crates of empty coca-cola bottles, and he doesn't need the help of that boy now. He sees me and stops for a chat.

"Where are you these days?" he asks me. "We hardly see you."

"I come often enough to Pumwani Informal School, but your barrow is never there, Stephen. You must be making lots of money; you seem to have plenty of work" I reply.

"No work, no food," he rejoins.

We occasionally meet one another at Pumwani School, which is more or less his base. If he has no work, he is there, lying on the barrow half asleep. He invariably asks whether I have a load for him, knowing well enough that I have none, but it is as good a way as any to start a conversation. That is how I came to know him. He is one of the seven hundred and fifty or so mostly young men who try to make a living by transporting goods by hand-barrow. Though he does not earn much, he manages to help his mother to pay the house rent. His intent is to own his own barrow, but he never seems to earn enough for that. He still rents this barrow from a boss who has six of them. A car hoots; Stephen is holding up the traffic so he moves on.

Around noon I drive along Juja Road, the big shopping 'avenue' of Mathare Valley, and it is lined with workshops, stalls, stands and small shops, all packed together. It is very crowded indeed. At one stall a woman sits knitting behind heaps of plastic bowls, jerry-cans, old and new, and tin cooking pots. Next to her there is a man who sells second-hand padlocks of dubious origin, as are the polished car hubcaps which hang on a rack in front of his stall, glittering in the sun. Beautiful pieces of cloth are out on display,

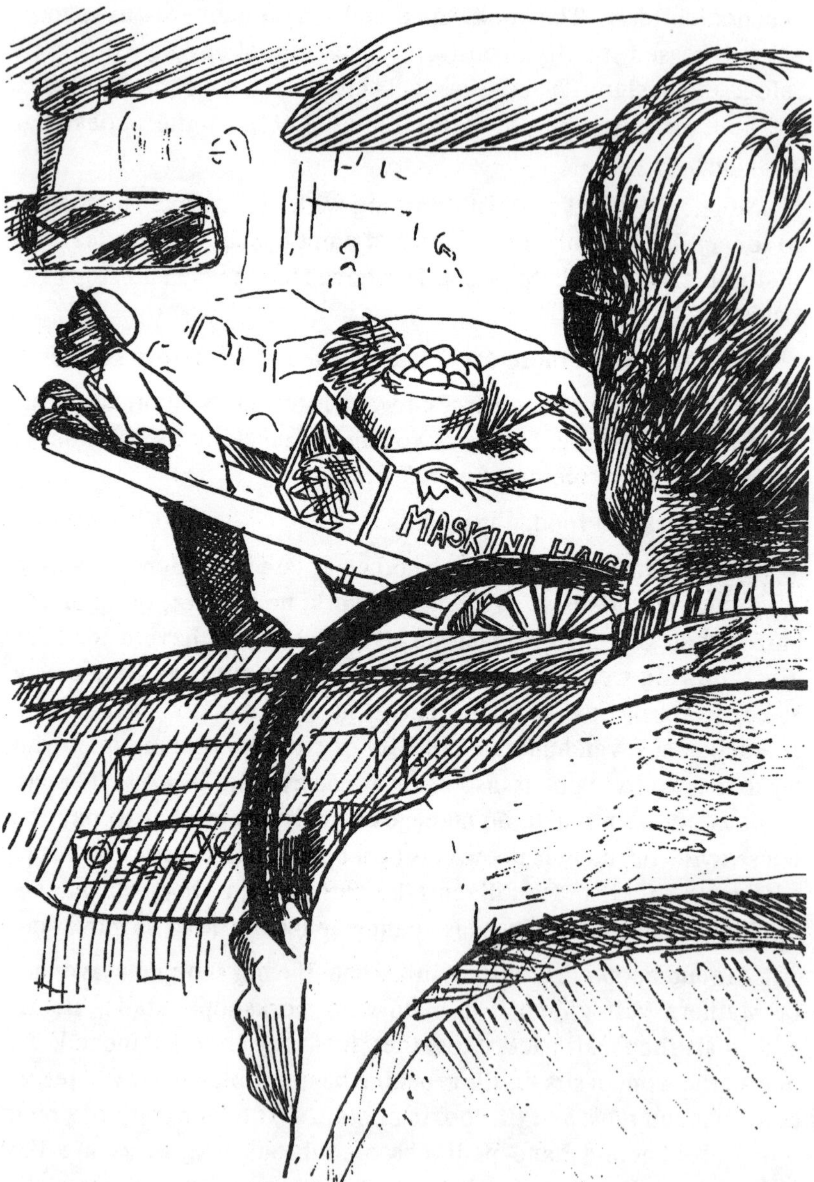
MASKINI HAICI

and so too is a good mattress made from the remains of two old ones. Above Martin's cobbler's shop is written in big letters, 'Undugu Shoes.' Years ago the Undugu Society gave him a loan to start his own small business, and he makes good shoes. A bit further along you can buy 'lorries'—sandals made from car tyres.

You can buy all kinds of beds: wrought-iron ones or beautiful wooden bedsteads with legs turned on a lathe. If you find these too expensive, go a little farther and you will find a place where you can buy a simple wooden frame criss-crossed with strips made from car inner-tubes.

The charcoal dealer is busy filling tins with a shilling's worth of charcoal. Goats and children scramble over the refuse heaps. Every place is jam-packed. The road is congested too, and I drift along with the rest of the torpid traffic. Cars, buses, lorries and matatus jostle for their piece of the road. Then suddenly I am behind that hand-barrow, *Maskini Haichoki*. I sound my horn, but Stephen doesn't turn his head; he is used to hooting drivers. The barrow is loaded with furniture—chairs, a bedstead and a mattress. A woman walks beside the barrow. When Stephen notices that it is me pestering him with the horn, he pulls his cart in front of me to block the way, then grinning, allows me to pass. It is hot at this time of the day. He has taken off his shirt and his skin glistens with sweat. He is a lean lad, but muscular. For a while he wanted to be a boxer, but after some practice he stopped. He was too tired in the evenings after work.

It is heavy work. He would be able to earn his living easily if it were regular, but every day is uncertain for there is plenty of competition. The only load he is sure of is the load of vegetables early in the morning for the women of Mathare Valley.

In the evening, after five o'clock, people in Eastleigh return from work or from 'tarmacking' (walking along the tarmac, looking for a job). Once again there are big crowds of men and many tired faces. Now, however, they are chatting to each other, no longer alone as they were this morning. Some carry cabbages or bundles of *Sikuma Weeki*,[6] bought for the evening meal, which, for most people is the only proper meal of the day. The cup of tea or plate of *uji* (maize porridge) they take during the day only keeps their stomachs quiet.

The mosque calls the people to prayer—in a little more personal manner than the cracked bells of St. Theresa's Church. Both the mosque and the church have enlisted the help of science. The voice from the mosque and the sound of bells have been recorded and are broadcast at fixed times at the push of a button. Several men go to the mosque for evening prayers. Others stop and listen to the preacher at the street corner who does not need a building, but who uses a battery-operated megaphone so that he can be heard above the noise around him.

The less devout make for their usual places in their favourite bars. All coffeehouses, bars, restaurants, day- and nightclubs are open at this time and business is brisk. The kiosks where cooked food is sold are also full of people. Radios and tape recorders blare out Congolese music. Here too you can hear *I'm Dreaming of a White Christmas,* sung by Jim Reeves in the middle of August. Some bars have a little butchery attached to them so that you can get a plate of roasted meat with your beer. But if you don't have a job you can only afford a roasted cob of maize, and it is very busy at the stalls selling these.

I stop my car to get some cigarettes at a little shop next to a bar called 'Suffering without Bitterness.' Then I see Stephen Waithaka passing by again. His barrow is loaded up with big sacks of unga flour. Two boys are helping him to push the huge load.

I call out to him, "Hey Stephen, you seem to have had a good day," He looks grim and tired.

"Eh," he says. He doesn't crack a smile.

Maskini haichoki —The poor don't get tired, is written on his barrow.

I wonder...

There is no man who cannot become an orphan. —KIKUYU PROVERB

HASSAN

"If Hassan can come today, we shall have a place for him, but then you must bring him here today without fail," the woman's emphatic voice informs me on the telephone.

That is all very well; but how will I be able to find Hassan if he isn't at home?

However carefully I drive, I cannot prevent the car from jolting as I enter Kitui Village. There is no good road here, but this is a nuisance only for me as the people of Kitui have no cars. Neither do they have latrines or running water. They have no sewers, no decent houses, and no work. They don't even have a good reputation. They are squatters on City Council land, a few thousand people in houses of cardboard and p.v.c. Sometimes Kitui is referred to as the 'cardboard city.' They don't have much, but despite, or perhaps because of their poverty, they do have a sense of community

Snotty-nosed children come up and greet me happily. Their mothers tell me that Hassan is somewhere around. Full of interest, they ask me if I have found a 'place' for him, and a few of them accompany me along the narrow pathways between the houses. I would not be able to find the house of Hassan's mother on my own although I have visited her several times already. The women tell me that his mother has gone away again—where, nobody knows. Now and again the neighbours give Hassan some food. Now Hassan must not wait for his mother, they tell me; this is his chance. He can go to school and he can learn. Everybody seems to be in favour of Hassan taking this opportunity. A small boy is lying half asleep beside one of the huts. An old coat, a few sizes too big, is draped over his body, his arm around a mangy dog as if it were his teddy bear. He looks at us with a sad, roguish face, it is like the face of an old man. This old man is six and he is Hassan. Getting up he stretches himself and looks inquiringly at me. I explain to him that there is a place for him in the home of which I have been talking during the past few months. A home where there is enough to eat, a home which has a roof that doesn't leak and a school with many other children. And what is even better, there are no jiggers.[8] Hassan starts scratching his sore toes; they are full of jiggers. He says nothing, only looks at me and smiles a bit

The people around me are happy and they ask whether the boy has to take something with him or not. Hassan shakes his head; what is there he could take along? He has nothing, not even a blanket. They ask if they should greet his mother for him, and he nods a Yes. "They can if the want"—it is all right with him. Then he takes my hand as if to say, "Let's go. I am finished with everything here." Hassan doesn't look back.

I try to talk with him but he keeps silent, moving his head in yes or no to my questions. I give him four pieces of chewing gum. The first three he swallows as he is very hungry. From the car he looks out carefully at everything, wondering at all the new streets, the cars and the people. I ask him whether he has seen his brother Shahu lately. Hassan silently shakes his head and looks out of the window all the more intently, as if Shahu might be somewhere around roaming the city.

Shahu is a few years older than Hassan. He has run away from home and now roves about the streets with other small boys, playing and stealing. Hassan has been along with Shahu a few times. He has slept with the others under plastic bags near the market. However, the other boys, eight and nine years old, considered him still a little kid, for he did not dare to steal. Their mother decided long ago that her boys were bad. She had decided that Hassan was bad before he was even six. We had discussed all this with the neighbours. No, children of six are not bad, but they do need a mother. Hassan's mother is seldom at home. She is often sick and she goes into town begging, not returning for days. At these times Hassan gets some food from the neighbours.

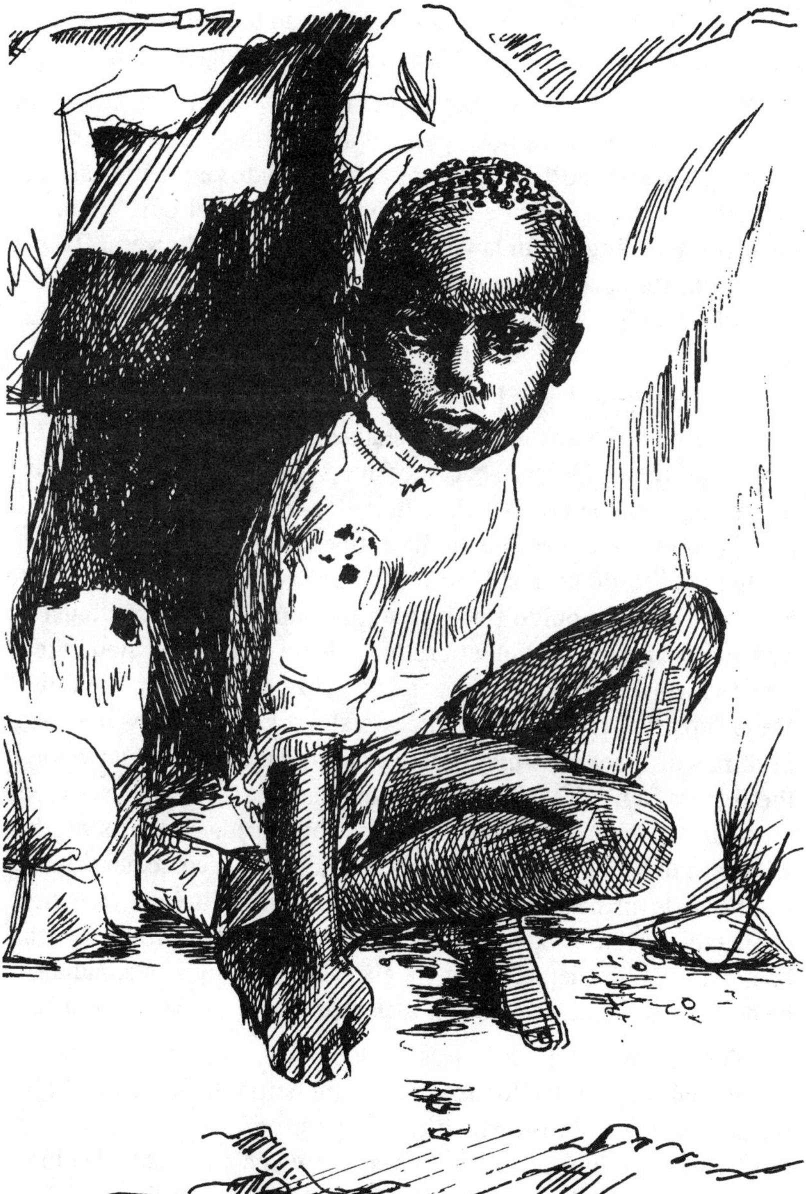

One day it was decided that we should try to find a home for Hassan, then perhaps the mother would be able to look after the two younger children. If Hassan was able to go to the children's home for a year, after that he could attend a school for neglected children.

We drive right to the other side of the city, to the rich side. The small boy sits with his nose pressed against the window, his eyes popping out, but still he says not a word. I drive slowly through the gates of the children's home, then stop and get out. There are beautiful buildings, trim lawns and many trees and flowers. Hassan stares and stares. He stays near the car, silent. When I tell him that he will be living here, he nods his head a little in agreement, not quite sure of himself. As we walk to the office he stops to stroke a toy giraffe, and his sad, roguish face comes to life with a smile.

A formidable social worker stands before Hassan, inspecting him carefully, and Hassan becomes number so-and-so. After a long pause she asks the boy whether he is Hassan, and Hassan nods. To me she says she hopes Hassan hasn't been roaming the streets yet, for then he would be a bad influence on the other children. I assure her that Hassan wouldn't do a thing like that and that she must be mixing him up with his elder brother, Shahu. I am very glad indeed now that Hassan remains quiet and doesn't pipe up with, "You liar." He is fidgeting on his chair. The social worker questions me about all kinds of diseases which Hassan might have. I only know about the jiggers in his feet. She decides that he will have to be scrubbed clean in the bath—probably the first bath in his life. His clothes will have to be burnt. I tell Hassan that he will get some new clothes and he nods his head to say that this is all right with him. Now he is eyeing this social worker very carefully indeed, and when she says that he must have his picture taken, he glances worriedly at me, but again he nods agreement. He no doubt feels that there is no way out of it.

Forms are filled while Hassan looks on. The photographer is called and they decide to take his picture before he is washed: later on they will be able to show the boy's progress the better. Once more he is scrutinized. Hassan appears very uncomfortable. He looks at us as if to say, "You lot haven't understood my problem at all."

At last he opens his mouth and declares, "I have to go for a pee."

There is a kind of man who is both foolish and wise. —MAASAI PROVERB

CHARLIE

This evening Charlie came round to see me. He comes quite often, a cheap guitar under his arm. His greeting is warm with a peculiar sad laugh to it, but unlike other Africans, he does not extend his hand to me. Charlie does not shake hands any more, "Whether you do or not, people still fight with one another," he says.

Those same people will tell you that Charlie is as mad as a hatter.

He falls on his knees before me and says, "Mathew, pray for me. Pray for my head so it will keep well for a couple of days, so that I can play my music."

Now I am not a terrific one for praying, but I suggest that we try it together. And so together we pray. We pray for a little light to enter that priceless, muddled head of Charlie. We also pray for his mother. She happens to be fine in the head, and so she feels the misery and poverty of her family all the more.

Charlie has to think so deeply before he can say anything that it is often difficult to talk with him. I have the impression that he thinks deep down into his stomach. He laughs about it himself. It is all because of that head of his, he knows.

It gets so bad at times that he starts preaching on the street corners about Jesus Christ. This happens especially when he is tired or when he has a lot on his mind. It is quite funny, and Charlie often laughs about it all, though he sometimes doesn't know exactly what he has been preaching about—but then (as I know) this also happens to many a priest.

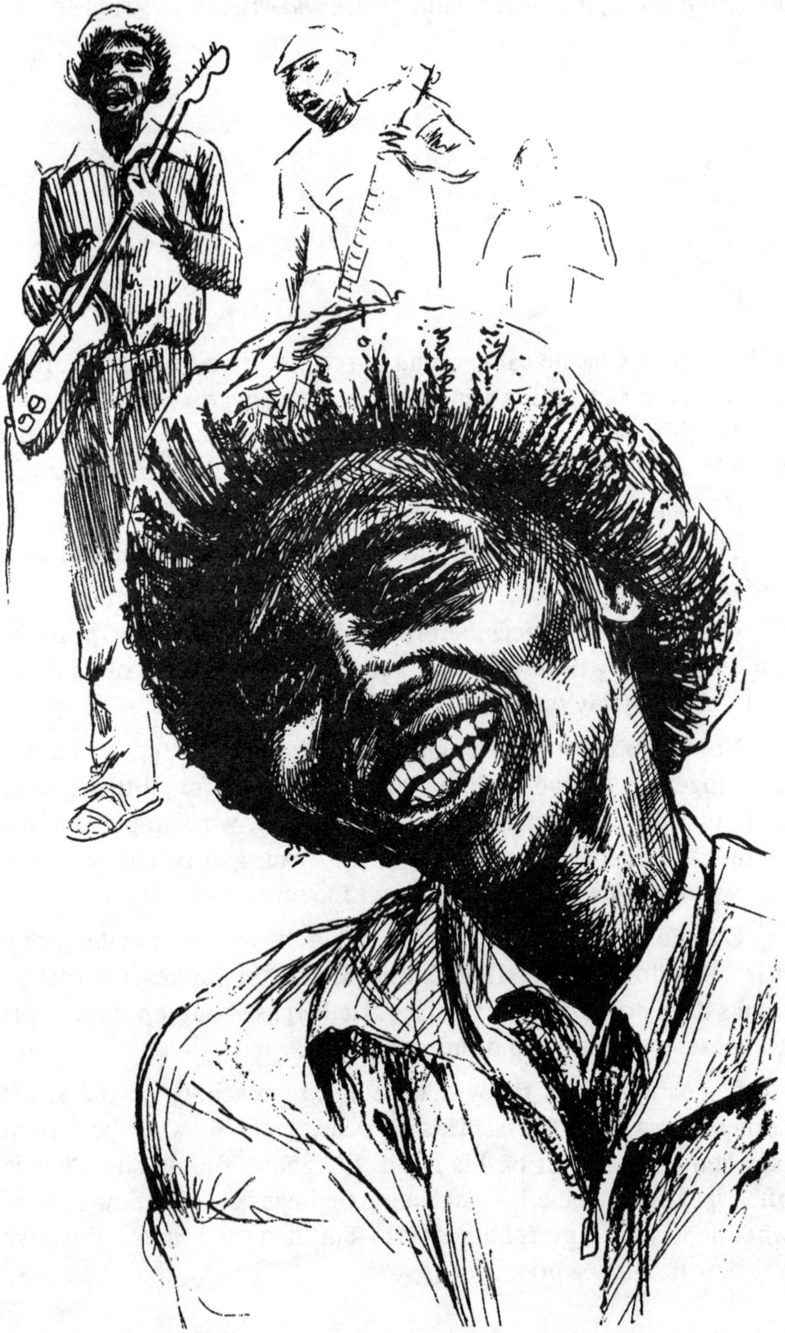

"At these moments I am sick," says Charlie. He looks at me dolefully and then he laughs again and says, "What am I supposed to do with a head like mine?"

I always enjoy Charlie's laugh; he laughs with his whole face. Then he reminds me of a clown. Yes, that Charlie, he's also a clown. In fact his name is not really Charlie; he was baptized James. But the people who saw him performing as a musician, a dancer, a clown, dubbed him Charlie. To them he was a great deal funnier than Charlie Chaplin. Charlie did not so much play his roles as live them. Yes, those were the days for him: Charlie and the people together. The applause, the people shouting "Encore!" And Charlie played, danced and sang. But like so many musicians, he started using drugs. He took them too freely and too often, and that was no good. This was the time that he started to have trouble with his head. Things went haywire. He even landed up in a psychiatric institution. "Never again," he says now. "It was like a madhouse in there."

Charlie is still thinking about his preaching. "Really a bit stupid," he reckons. But then he looks at me; he is very serious. "They just don't understand about this Jesus and his people. I mean Jesus, the Son of God, being with ordinary people, just like that. They don't get it. Kings call on Kings, the President doesn't just go visiting any old beggar."

According to Charlie, it was the most understandable thing in the world that the Pope did not visit Mathare Valley when he came to Kenya. I had hoped that it would be possible; Charlie had no such expectations. At least that is what he says, but he sings a different tune.

For Charlie, singing is easier than talking, and he reaches for his guitar. Then, with closed eyes, he sings about his own particular kind of sovereign, his 'Queen.' This queen is truly his own, his dream. In this song, which he composed, a queen goes to visit the poor folks. She goes alone, she talks with them, she eats their food, she dances with the people and she listens attentively to what they have to say about their lives. Charlie sings it with his whole soul. I listen and it strikes me that Charlie doesn't sing about his queen bringing lots of presents.

He finishes his song and looks up at me.

"That is a beautiful song, Charlie."

"Yes," he says, "It is a beautiful song because I wrote it myself."

Then he becomes sad again because people just do not act like that, or so it seems to him. "Only this Jesus, eh?—He was like my queen, he was on the side of the poor," murmurs Charlie. "But it only goes to show that he was God as well," he adds.

I think that Charlie tends to hold too dim a view of people, and I tell him so. Charlie shakes his head sadly, "No, people don't really love people. God is the only one who loves people."

We keep talking, searching. Has Charlie, then, never truly experienced love, I wonder. "Are people really so bad?" I ask.

Charlie thinks... he thinks so very deeply. "No," he says, "I don't say that people are bad...but..."

He cannot express himself properly. But he is willing to sing about that difficulty, too. His whole philosophy of life is in his songs. So he tries to tune his guitar, but it is not so easy, and it takes time because one of the strings is a bit worn. "It needs a new one," says Charlie, "but that costs money."

Then when his guitar is reasonably in tune, with a smiling face and a sad voice, he sings,

> If you had sufficient
> And I just enough
> Then we would never hate one another,
> We would live in peace and love.

I listen, full of admiration. Maybe the true theologians are walking in the streets and aren't sitting behind desks writing books.

I ask myself what this 'sufficient' might be, and what 'just enough' is. In any case, it is more than Charlie has right now.

"Perhaps then we can come to love all the other people..." he sings.

And then everything is quiet; we are both still thinking of the words. I ask myself when this so-called half-wit thinks all this out.

We talk some more and Charlie answers my question in his next song. Sometimes everything is very, very quiet, and very clear in that head of his. 'The noon of the night,' Charlie calls it in his song.

Now, as he sings, his voice is almost a whisper, and his guitar is whispering too. Charlie is singing about the noon of the night, when all is still in its quiet depths. Then you can see your pain for what it is, but you can experience happiness at the same time. Then things become clearer. Then you can sing. Such is the time when Charlie writes his songs and ballads.

As he puts down his guitar once again, he says, "It is good of you to listen to my songs; most people don't, they only want to hear about broken love affairs."

Not knowing what to do or what to say, I give Charlie some money to buy a new string for his guitar. Often we Europeans are so poor that we can give only money. He gets up right away to go and buy it.

I ask him how his head is now. He feels it with his hand, gives me his laughing wink, and taps his head as if to say, "Touch wood!"

Charlie is as mad as a hatter—so people say. . . .

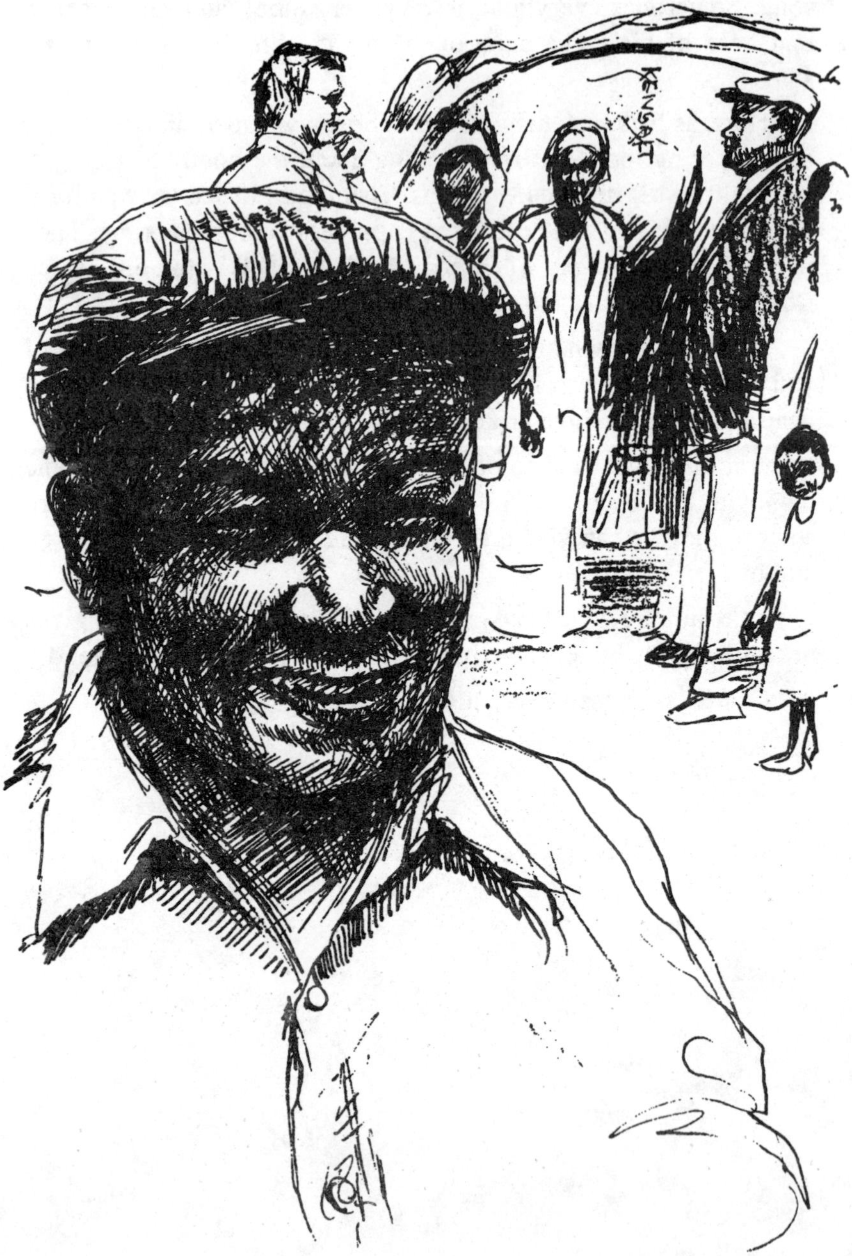

*He who seeks his goat with the man who ate it,
is certain not to find it.* —KIKUYU PROVERB

THE FREEDOM FIGHTER

Njoroge isn't really drunk, but he has certainly had a few. Others might say that he has had a few too many, but I know Njoroge can hold his drink.

He invites me to sit down and offers me an empty tin to sit on. When Njoroge is in a drinking mood, he is also in the mood for a serious talk. He is an impressive man as he sits here with his sturdy face in front of his hovel of polythene and cardboard.

He offers me a glass of chang'aa, but I refuse. A wise thing to do, he opines. Quite deadly, this chang'aa which he brews himself on the banks of Nairobi River. "'Kill me quick,' we call it," Njoroge says, and he takes another glass. Njoroge is one of the many unlicensed brewers of chang'aa. It gives him a little extra income, that is, when he doesn't have to bribe the police.

But tonight Njoroge has started to drink himself. It makes him feel less hungry and you forget the misery around you, or sometimes you see it more sharply. The misery is great here in Kirinyagga Village, where Njoroge acts as a village leader. In huts of polythene and cardboard two hundred and twenty-five families are trying to survive. I say 'families,' but they are very incomplete families. Most consist of unmarried, divorced or separated women, with several children. It looks a bit like women's emancipation gone haywire. Many of these women came to town looking for jobs and looking for some independence. They didn't find either, and some of them ended up as prostitutes. Now a little older and discouraged, they try to survive in Kirinyagga. We call their hovels 'igloos,' since they resemble the dwellings of the Eskimos. But don't think of coolness, for it is stifling hot under the polythene and there is no ventilation whatsoever.

Here, Njoroge is the village boss. There is a village committee, but everybody recognizes Njoroge as their leader. He is an understanding man who settles quarrels and sees to it that the poor among the poor get something to eat.

But tonight he feels 'down.' He doesn't know exactly whether he is down because he has been drinking or whether he is drinking because he feels so down.

He tells stories about the fifties, when he was a freedom fighter. Yes, Njoroge was a fighter. He fought for the freedom of Kenya, for his country, for his land, a piece of land where he could live with his wife, his children, a few cows and a goat. He didn't fight alone. He fought together with the famous Mau Mau[9] fighters. "I was in prison, five long years," Njoroge says, and then somewhat scornfully, "A famous man was imprisoned, also for five long years. The famous man was freed first. I was let out of prison a few months later. We got *Uhuru* (freedom, independence). The famous man became President; he was my friend."

Njoroge talks on while he fills his glass again. "No, no chang'aa for me," I decline his offer.

He tells me how jubilantly he celebrated Uhuru, together with many other freedom fighters. He even shook hands with the famous man. He was sure that he would soon get his piece of land, the land which the famous man and he had fought for. He didn't know whether it was a question of weeks or of months. Yes, he was patient. He waited for years, living in an old shack in Pumwani. He got a job as a night watchman; he wasn't afraid. He was a man with guts. He was guarding one of the buildings of the City Council when his own hut, together with many others, was bulldozed away during the night by the same City Council. New houses which only the rich could afford would be built there.

"Wicked, isn't it?" he says.

"Very wicked indeed," I reply.

Njoroge was angry then, and that was when he became the leader of these abandoned and dejected people. He collected his few possessions and with many others, he built this settlement of Kinyago. That was more than ten years ago. He encouraged the people; nobody was going to chase them away again. Hadn't he fought for land? And the City Council would listen this time.

Njoroge has been to see many people in many offices—a piece of land for him and his people, a piece of land where they could settle, build decent huts, where they would not be driven away again. That has been Njoroge's fight now for years. All to no avail it seems. But during the last elections Njoroge saw a new chance. "Our votes for a plot of land where we can stay," he said to one of the candidates. The support of Njoroge was important during the election campaign. The candidate knew that, and he didn't say no to Njoroge, but he didn't quite say yes either.

Anyway, Njoroge had new hope. "But then..." He pours some more burning chang'aa down his throat. "But then, those stupid women became jubilant when they received a piece of dress material from the candidate. That politician knew he had won their votes, and I knew that we would never get that piece of land."

"Those stupid women," he says again, shaking his head sadly.

He laughs scornfully and looks around. No piece of land, no cow, no goat, no trees or grass that he can call his own. Only this scraggy dog is his. He wonders whether he is still an African.

"I was imprisoned and that famous man was imprisoned."

Yes, for *him* things took a better turn. No, Njoroge isn't jealous that he didn't become President himself. Only one can be the President, and this famous man was a good man. But then, these thousands of acres of land, the many houses, the best cows. Why is all this in the hands of a few? Njoroge hasn't even seen it, but he knows it is true.

"Weren't we fighting for the same freedom, for the same land?" Njoroge asks slowly.

No, Njoroge isn't an embittered man, but he feels sad about it all. Again he offers me a glass of chang'aa. He fills the glass from a plastic bottle which looks filthy. "Take a swig," he says. "Most people survive it."

Then whilst he looks around this overcrowded settlement once more, "Those stupid women."

I have not said much tonight; I only listened to Njoroge. But now I accept his glass and I take a sip. It burns like hell.

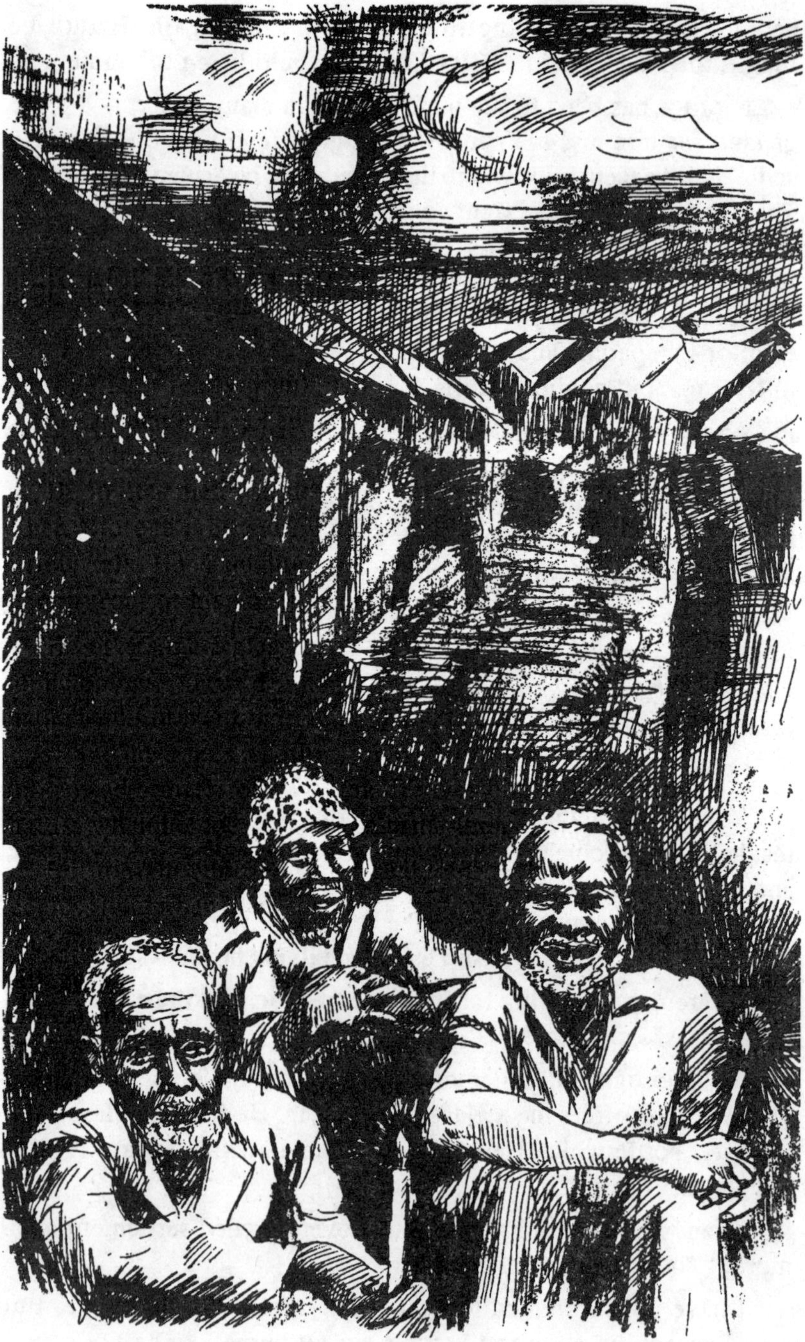

Great events may stem from words of no importance. —Zaire proverb

A LIGHT IN THE DARKNESS

"*Mzungu! mzungu!*" (a white man! a white man!)[10] a few children shout as I do my utmost not to step in the open sewer. I try my flashlight again, but the batteries are dead.

Two women guide me. They live here in Mathare Valley. They know the way, all the little paths between the shacks—there are hardly any real roads in the Valley. They talk ahead of me, weaving through this enormous village where more than eighty thousand people live, or at least, try to survive. The houses are of scrap wood with roofs of polythene, galvanized iron or old tins. They are packed together and lean on one another propping each other up. There are a few street lights in Mathare Valley, but they are no help to me on these narrow paths between the houses.

"Watch out, here is a gutter," one of the women warns. I don't see it, but I smell it. Small hand-made lamps light the houses and there are a few lanterns as well. It all looks a bit ghostly.

I am getting used to the darkness now and I start to see that the shadows around me are people. Men talk together in front of the tea kiosk. Women cook the evening meal on charcoal stoves. Children and radios screech and a couple of drunks try to convince one another that life is beautiful. Mathare Valley is a crowded place, but it still has something of a village atmosphere about it.

We knock on the door of a Luo[11] family. They have asked us to call—they want to talk about the blessing of their marriage. We enter a small room divided in two by a plastic curtain. Here the Ouma family lives. We are welcomed with extensive greetings. There is a lot of commotion to get a few stools together from under the bed and from the neighbours, so we can all sit down.

Ouma's wife talks a lot; she has a husband, she has three children, she is a Catholic and wants to marry in church. Her husband is not a Catholic, but he wants to be a Catholic. She has arranged everything, in spite of the fact that it is thought women have nothing useful to say.

Ouma himself is very quiet. He doesn't deny that he wants to become a Catholic, but he is obviously relieved when I explain that I am willing to bless their marriage even if he doesn't become one. Yes, he finds this blessing important all right; a marriage feast would be too expensive. But he would certainly like God's blessing on their life here in Mathare Valley. Since they get nobody else's blessing, they value God's blessing all the more. Time and time again people ask, "Will you bless us, pray with us, father?" We pray together, they in Luo, I in my faulty Swahili.[12]

Then we move on, walking very close to the houses in order to avoid the gutter in the middle of the path. We more or less slide to our next address.

"*Hodi, hodi,*—We're here, anyone home?" One of my guides calls in front of the door of Titus and Maria Magdalena. After some shuffling of chairs and the removal of a padlock, the door opens. Again, a very warm welcome. We shake hands with people whom we can hardly see in the dim light of the oil lamp. Two small children sit on the floor with a plate of ugali (maize cake). They look baffled at a white man entering their house. They extend their sticky hands with obvious apprehension; their mother has to encourage them before they will risk it.

We talk together, first about important things: the weather, life in the Valley, parents at home. In discussing the latter, it turns out that Magdalena was baptized by Father Walstra, who was my parish priest years ago. Our visit then becomes a family reunion. In that case I should also know Magdalena's sister who lived next to the mission. Of course I know her sister. I even remember the name of her husband. They bring in a pot of tea, with too much milk to my liking, and we talk about their life here. It transpires that I am a very good friend of theirs; twenty minutes ago we were still strangers.

The couple feel that they are blessed, living with their two children in this shack. A poster for Lady Gay (a body lotion) hangs on the wall; beneath it the slippers of Magdalena hang on a nail. A wire strung out above the bed serves as a wardrobe.

They consider that after all these years here together they are sufficiently married to admit this in church. "Titus tries to find work and isn't drunk very often," Maria Magdalena says—additional reasons to have their union blessed.

I write down their names. When I ask for their address, Titus says with a snigger, "W.C. 142." I think it is a joke, but he is serious. The numbered toilets of the City Council are the only recognizable points you can use to find somebody in this neighbourhood. There are no street names, no house numbers, no nameplates; everybody lives here anonymously. Only the toilets are numbered.

After a promise that we will visit them again, we go to our next appointment. With my colleague, John Slinger, we have agreed to baptize three old men at home. We had decided to make a simple ceremony of it at their home, without all the bustle. At least that is what John and I intended, but when we arrive, there are fifty people sitting together in an open spot between the houses. The Christians of the neighbourhood have decided that this is going to be a big feast. Baptism is not a personal matter; it is a matter for the whole community. There is applause when we arrive—now the ceremony can start.

The three old men sit on chairs, their heads shaven. There are chairs for John and myself and a lantern which gives out just enough light to read the Bible. People start to sing, accompanied by a guitar. A girl comes running with a tambourine; now it sounds even better.

The baptism ceremony which happens is not exactly what is in the liturgy book. The symbolism of water and light becomes far more meaningful here in the Valley, where there are hardly any stand-pipes and where the people have no electric light. Perhaps we have become too accustomed to such amenities to appreciate them fully.

Baptism acquires a new meaning for me too. A few pieces of candle are lit with difficulty and are blown out by the wind.

Relighting them becomes part of the ceremony: in everyday life it can be difficult to keep the light burning too. There is a strong wind against the light, most certainly here in Mathare Valley. One of the old men carefully shields the light in his hand; he really wants to keep it burning.

We talk about the Church they want to enter, not a church of stone, but a Church of people. They are the Church as they sit here together under the moonlit sky. They make big promises, these three old men, and the people promise to support them in all this.

Together we pray. Some of the prayers are long, from mothers with many cares and worries; then there is a quick prayer of a child that she may pass her primary school examinations. People sing again and clap their hands. The three newly baptized are congratulated by everybody. In their old age they are as happy as small children. Three bottles of lemonade are brought out for the baptized and the two baptizers. We raise our glasses and drink together whilst the others sing and dance.

It is late when we leave the Valley in the company of a few people. Two policemen who have just entered the Valley notice us: two white men here so late. They ask whether anybody has given us any trouble. "No, nobody gave us trouble."

A little shrub may grow into a tree. —Sudanese proverb

THE SEWING GROUP

Bibiana didn't ask for work any more; she only asked to be helped. She looked miserable and defeated by life in Kinyago. We asked what she could do to earn a little money for herself and her children. "I can't do anything," she answered.

Maybe she had been told too often that she was good-for-nothing. She looked at the ground while her hands were busy with some crochet work. Wouldn't she like to try to join the women's group and do some crochet work there? Then she would be able to earn a bit of money. Her answer was a very timid "yes," not at all convincing. Diana, a volunteer who works with the women's group, encouraged her and discussed it with her.

Lea was living in the same village, Kinyago, when she joined the sewing group a few years ago. More precisely, she has lived just outside this illegal settlement of huts made of p.v.c. and cardboard. She had found a man whom she was willing to call her husband, and she lived with him and a few children in a small room in Eastleigh Section III. However, her whole family lived in Kinyago and she was considered one of 'Kinyago' when she looked for work. When she was asked what she could do, her answer was not as timid as Bibiana's. "I can do anything, and what I don't know, I can learn," was her answer.

Bibiana and Lea joined this women's group of Undugu at about the same time. The group had started more or less accidentally with women like Lea and Bibiana who were looking for work. There is no work, but these women are good with their hands. Some were knitting pullovers for school uniforms, which Undugu would buy for their school sponsorship programme. Others were making dolls and stuffed toys, however, these were hard to sell. Some of the women didn't care much about quality—the only thing they seemed to be interested in was money. They left the whole organization of the project to Diana, the volunteer. Women like Lea grabbed as much work as they could for themselves; they were able to take more work than the others as they fought harder to get it. People like Bibiana made do with what was left, which wasn't much.

A week later the women would throw badly-finished articles on the table and demand money. A lot of quarreling and shouting went on, and Diana and Eddah of Undugu (another helper) felt like screaming.

Something had to be done. Some of the people who were working with the women, the director of Undugu and I, who worked in the villages where the women came from, sat down and put our heads together. We discussed quality and marketing and we talked about self-reliance. We decided that the women needed some training. Would the women be prepared to come three mornings a week? Would six weeks be too long? Should they be formed into smaller groups so that they could run their own affairs better?

The women were more enthusiastic than we had expected. For six weeks they came three mornings a week to the Mennonite Centre in Eastleigh. These were women from Pumwani, Kitui, Kinyago and a few from Mathare Valley. The Mennonite Centre was neutral ground. Everybody had to walk quite a distance to get there. Joke van Asseldonk, one of the advisers, had designed a simple blouse with crochet work, which was easier to sell than dolls and stuffed toys. We had several volunteers who instructed the women, but in many ways they instructed one another. People like Bibiana were encouraged, and women like Lea were told 'where to get off' by the other women.

The course ended with a two-day workshop. Everyone discussed how they lived, how they stayed alive, how they could improve their own situation. Lea spoke up in front of the whole group. Bibiana dared only to express herself before the small groups, but there the others saw that her views were quite sound. The women wanted to start a savings scheme but only within each small group, as it was hard for people from Kinyago to trust people from Kitui. After all, they didn't live together.

So the sewing group started its own life—a spin-off from the knitting group. New designs were made. Diana and Sister Janet, who had come to work with us, searched for markets. Gradually, the women got to know one another. They were becoming organized. They realized that though they had been acquainted for a long time, they did not properly understand one another. Eventually they formed a firm group with Lea in the foreground and Bibiana somewhere in the background.

Sister Janet started to visit the women at home in Kinyago. They no longer talked solely about money although there were always some who begged for more than they had earned. They started talking about their own lives, about their community, about the lack of water, the stealing, the drinking, the bribery and the baptism of their children. They asked about religion, about this whole 'Christianity thing,' and they told sister Janet that they wanted to be baptized. Nobody would have considered forming a sewing group as evangelization, but maybe it was all part of the process. To some it gave hope, for others it definitely was 'good news.' Bibiana was encouraged by the fact that people wanted to pray together; she wouldn't have dared to suggest it herself.

Lea decided that she wanted to be baptized. If she had been baptized before, she had forgotten about it. I am glad that she has not been converted so much that she can no longer fight. She still fights, though now not only for herself, but for the whole group.

Things still don't go smoothly all the time, and tempers still flare up when the women come together to divide the work on Fridays. Luckily, it is no longer up to Diana to control them. As their leader, Lea might now put all the clothes into the cupboard and say, "No more work for this week, until you decide that you can behave." The women accept it grudgingly. After all, they formally chose Lea as their leader a few months ago, she having been the unofficial leader for some time. A leader in Africa usually has a fair amount of power. Bibiana supports Lea. Bibiana is the one who irons the made-up dresses on Friday mornings, and she has seen for herself that some of the dresses are not finished properly. She dares to speak up these days, knowing that she is worth something—and she is respected.

The sewing group no longer makes just simple blouses; now it markets a whole range of very fine dresses which the women themselves, however, would not wear. They sell them in the boutiques in town. They have their own trademark, too—*Orembo* (which means *Beautiful*). They also have their own revolving fund. The group asked Undugu for a loan of thirty thousand Kenya shillings and got it. In this way it has become more self-reliant, although marketing remains a bit of a problem, for shops are willing to buy but are not prepared to pay cash.

Many good things happen. For instance, when some blankets for destitute old people were stolen from Diana's car whilst she was helping at the sewing group, the women, who a few years ago could think only about themselves, organized a very good collection to buy some new blankets. Diana is no longer the 'employer' but has gradually assumed an advisory role. The women are taking many of the organizational responsibilities into their own hands, and in doing so become more involved in their own community. It has taken a few years for things to change. Altogether, more than a hundred women are in the women's groups. Lea leads the sewing group with about thirty members. They each earn between one hundred and one hundred-and-fifty Kenya shillings a week—about the official minimum wage in Kenya, which certainly is not paid to many people in East Nairobi. With so much unemployment, many are prepared to work for less.

If there is a crisis (and there seems to be one every few weeks) we no longer have to hold a meeting. The women sort it out between themselves. Thieving is still going on, and usually it is the sewing cottons and materials that are taken. Methods for dealing with this are not always pleasant. For instance, the group decided that everybody's handbag would have to be checked before leaving the centre. Who was trustworthy enough? Who was not a thief herself? Bibiana was appointed unanimously. Other measures have been taken regarding the quality of the goods produced. Everybody hands her work to Lea and another woman who check it before it is paid for. Quality is especially important now, because though you might not credit it, Orembo, the 'beautiful' group, is about to begin exporting their dresses to the parish of Sancta Maria in Stuttgart, Germany. The women are very proud of this.

Lea says, "That is very clever of us, isn't it?"

Bibiana says, "It is very kind of these people to help us and buy our dresses."

If you offend, ask for pardon, if offended, forgive. —Ethiopian proverb

PAGAN JUSTICE

I am thoroughly fed up! For months we have been working to start a fund for these women. It would have made them independent, able to stand on their own feet. As a group of traditional dancers, they had opened their own savings account and all the members were paying in money.

They dance their traditional dances for the President. They dance on national feast days, at weddings and at political meetings. These women dance well. In the dance they come to life. No, this is not a young girls' group. Most of the members are mature women who become young again in the trance of the dance. They enjoy it immensely, but what is also important to these mothers without jobs or husbands, is that they earn some money doing it.

They were going to save this money, put it in the bank and leave it there until it was really needed for a hawker's license or school uniforms for their children. Several of the women earn their food by hawking vegetables. Now with collective funds they would be able to buy vegetables more cheaply, and they would make a better profit, perhaps even earn a living instead of a mere subsistence. It took a long time and a lot of talking and no little trust before everything was settled. Nyamira was elected and duly appointed as treasurer. She knows about business and she can count.

But now this big mess, and everything has collapsed. Nyamira has used the money for her own business. She saw a chance to buy rice on the black market, but she didn't have six hundred shillings in cash. She took the money from the women's group. Perhaps she meant to refund it. Perhaps she thought it would be only for a few days.

But this time her black market deal misfired and she went bankrupt. The money has gone. And I, I had so much confidence in Nyamira. And the women, they had hoped so fervently that they would succeed this time with their fledgling credit union. I find it terribly unjust. If a project fails, it often takes years before the people dare to start again.

Now we are here together with the village committee to discuss the matter. It is a public meeting in one of the dirty slums of Nairobi. Everybody is entitled to hear what is being discussed. The dance group represents the whole community; its problems concern the whole community. The women are busy weaving their sisal bags. They sit on stones or old tins. Others just sit on the ground. Nyawira was here half an hour ago. She greeted me today with a stony face and went away. She does not belong at the meeting.

The whole situation is explained once more. Some are very angry with Nyamira—I can understand that. Others laugh scathingly, they never trusted Nyawira. Even now they are not so sure about her—maybe she has hidden the money somewhere. There is an atmosphere of loss and defeat; they had hoped so much this time they would succeed. What were they to do? Make a new start? Many think that it will be of no use. Should we make a police case of it? Not many react to that proposal. Make Nyamira pay back the money? Useless, she will cheat them again, they think. Moreover, how would she be able to refund the money? She obviously has none. Her only trade at the moment is in bones, which she sells to a glue factory for a few shillings a load.

I listen. Sometimes I am at a loss to understand these people. A chicken thief is beaten to death. Now someone steals six hundred shillings from the community; they feel defeated and say, "This kind of thing will happen again." It is especially this last point—that it will happen again and again—which is so discouraging. People lose the confidence to persevere. I listen and I feel frustrated.

Then they ask for my opinion, and in my frustration I take up the proposal to make a police case of it. Only few people agree; others reject the proposal. Nyamira would go to jail; she has no money to repay.

"All right, let her go to jail for a while. It will be a lesson for her, and for others too. Perhaps it will prevent people stealing from their own community in future." I am incensed with our ex-treasurer when I say this.

"But we ourselves appointed her," says one woman as if this makes her an accomplice in the theft.

I try to explain again that we shall never make any real progress if someone can steal from the community and get away with it. People will get more and more discouraged, and corruption, which is bad enough as it is, will only increase. Where will it end? It is especially vexing here where the money was stolen from very poor people.

Only a few young people, perhaps wanting to take revenge, nod some kind of agreement. Then the old Mugo looks at me. He is an ancient with a wrinkled face, but his youthfulness has never left him. He is a friend of mine and has told me much about the customs of the Kikuyu tribe. Mugo isn't a Christian; the traditional African religion is good enough for him. He is still what in the past we would have called 'a pagan,' and they are becoming rare these days, certainly in Nairobi. But Mugo always joins us when we celebrate Mass together in this community.

This old Mugo looks at me and waits until the women are silent, and he speaks, "We know that you Europeans are very clever," he says. "You made motorcars and even the aeroplane in which you came. You brought us books. You, yourself, you work for God and you know many things about God. It is good that you came here to pray with our people."

"He comes to celebrate Mass," says a woman who is a Catholic.

"It is good that you came to pray with our people," Mugo repeats, as if he has nothing to do with that Mass business. "I have listened a few times, and you prayed something like this, 'Forgive us our trespasses as we forgive those who trespass against us.'"

"You see," Mugo says, "That is what I find so clever with you Europeans; you can forgive someone and yet you throw him or her into prison. How do you combine these two?"

Silence... Mugo nods at me kindly as if to say, "I don't want to be personal." The people look at me, wondering how I am going to answer that one. My first reaction is the word "justice" which has to be done. For us, justice is frequently the greatest virtue. But this pagan talks about more. He talks about not writing-off people, about making the journey together, whatever happens. He has told me before that hardly anyone is ever thrown out of the traditional community. Is that perhaps the real love about which Christ speaks?

A bit sheepishly I admit that we Europeans are not all that clever after all. I withdraw my proposal to make a police case. No, I don't know the solution to the problem we are discussing here. But what I do know is that we should start listening to these few 'pagans' who are still around. They are an endangered species. Still, they can convert us.

It is better to be poor than to be sick. —HAYA PROVERB

THE WITCH DOCTOR

Sara is lying on her bed of old rags. The air in her hut is stifling; there is hardly any ventilation. She is thin and haggard, gasping for breath and nearly dying again. I have brought some medicine which I hope will relieve her asthma a little. Sara has been suffering from asthma for years and she looks worn out, skin and bones. She is a frail little woman at the best of times. When she is up and about she ekes out some sort of existence knitting sweaters for school children. There are usually a few children staying with her, but I never know which are her own.

The nurse who gave me the medicine for Sara understood when I told her how badly Sara was suffering. She explained that in the end the medicine would affect the heart, and unless treated in hospital the invalid would probably die. But Sara doesn't want to go to hospital any more. She seems to know that she is going to die. Still, she is not resigned to death. Though her body is very weak, she remains a spirited woman. Sara tells me that the tablets we bring her give only a little relief and that her heart hurts. Our medicine doesn't really cure her; it is not like the Kamba medicine that once saved her.

The village leader who is with me, speaks English and knows the European ways. He brushes aside this witch doctor nonsense. He knows that Sara wants to go and see a traditional doctor, but he also knows that generally we missionaries are not great fans of the traditional medicine. Sara remains calm and explains again that the traditional doctor cured her once and the European medicine never cured her. She calls the Kamba doctors *daktari ya kunyegi*—traditional doctors, and not witch doctors.

I explain to Sara that Western medicine and traditional medicine often don't mix. She accepts that; she is willing to stop taking the Western medicine for a few weeks before she takes the traditional medicine. And then she adds that she wants 300 Kenya shillings from me, the fee for the traditional doctor. I must admit I do not have much confidence in this medicine man of whom I know nothing. As far as I am concerned, Sara can try the witch doctor now that she is going to die anyway, but I am rather hesitant to be an accomplice in her folly. I would at least like to speak to this *daktari* first.

I am surprised when somebody says, "We can go and call her right now and you can speak to her." In a little while they return with an unassuming old mama. I had expected an impressive figure, perhaps wearing some dangling gourds and other paraphernalia. But I know this woman; I have seen her selling vegetables. Is she going to beat all these famous pharmaceutical companies in curing Sara's asthma? We talk. Yes, she thinks she can cure Sara; she can bring the right medicine from Kamba country. But a certain cloth has to be bought and she will have to pay for the medicine too. I still feel uncomfortable at paying for the treatment, and formulate my objection.

Sara and the others know my brother; he has visited them in the past. "If I need help from my brother, do you think he will help me, if he has the means?" I ask.

"Of course he will. He is your brother," they answer.

"Could I come to you to ask for money to pay my brother?" They all laugh; that indeed would be ridiculous.

Sara looks at the old woman who feels a bit uneasy about it all. She is of the same clan as Sara. Could she see Sara as her own sister? "But your doctors charge a lot of money as well," she says.

"They sure do, but we haven't charged Sara for the medicine we brought her."

People start discussing the matter and I leave them to it. Things are still vague when I go.

As I drive away I wonder about all these *waganga*[13] in Nairobi. In eastern Nairobi in particular, hundreds of them are consulted every day. Their clients are mostly the poor, but the rich sometimes visit them too. Some of them are quacks who exploit the people, but then so do many doctors who practice Western medicine and have their clinics in Eastleigh. Maybe these waganga are the psychiatrists of Kenya. The people in our area live under circumstances which would drive anybody insane. When the child is sick, the mother takes the child to see the medicine man. He starts by treating the mother, I am told. Not such a bad approach.

Anyway, in the case of Sara, we have nothing to lose since she will soon die unless she finds some miracle treatment. Still, I am glad that I haven't paid the three hundred shillings.

A car in front of me boasts that Cafenol cures all your pains. These people live in a strange world: a mixture of traditional ways and Western ways. They really don't mix very well.

Three weeks have passed, and this morning I met Sara carrying a debe (bucket) of water. The last time I saw her she could hardly carry her wool and knitting needles. She looks as thin as ever, but she is breathing and she smiles; she is alive again. I am really pleased. Yes, the medicine worked, she tells me. Even so, she now wants a European doctor to give her a check-up to see whether the sickness has really gone. She knows they can look inside; the traditional doctors can't do that. She doesn't talk about the doctor's fee any more and I am wise enough not to ask.

Nevertheless, Sara does have a problem. She earns only a few shillings by knitting, and that is barely enough to keep herself and the children alive. Now she would like to send one of the children back to 'the reserve,' to go to school. She can stay with her grandmother. We have said so often that the rural areas are better for children than this slum. The only problem is the 300 Kenya shillings for the school uniform. Would Undugu be so kind as to help out in this case? I am inclined to think that there is a very good possibility. The child will have a better chance to grow up healthily in the countryside rather than in the misery here. I can't promise anything, but I tell Sara that I will definitely recommend her case to Undugu. She is happy about that.

As I drive along to visit some people in Pumwani, I wonder which of Sara's children is of school age. I am not sure which are her children. I don't want to raise any false hopes. Are those children staying with her really her children? She did ask for money for a uniform, but I have my doubts. I have a feeling that the three hundred shillings will be for the traditional doctor and not a school uniform!

I am learning to live with my doubts about African ways and Western ways.

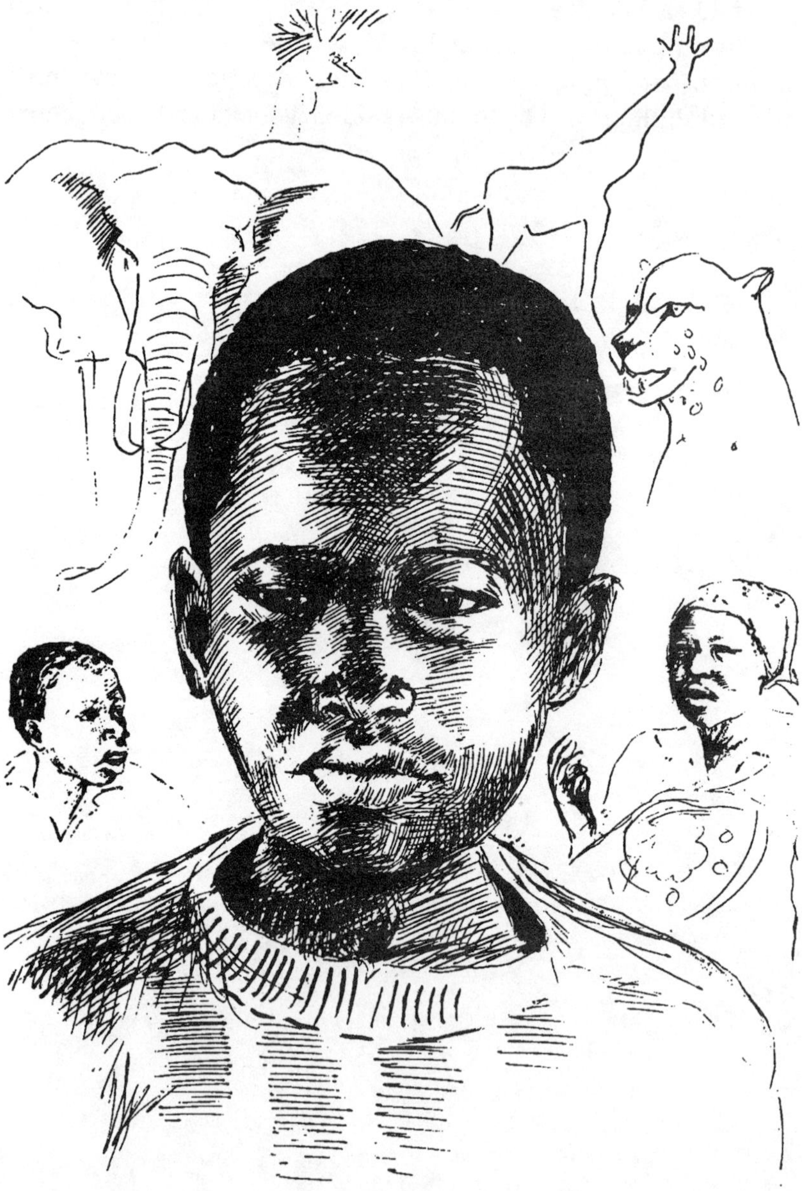

Half a loaf is better than no bread. —ZULU PROVERB

SON KASUKI

Kasuki has a bit of a slouch when he walks and he has told me that I don't walk particularly upright either. I know that isn't exactly a compliment, but Kasuki can tell me such things because we have agreed to be friends, and in friendships less complimentary things can be mentioned.

When I first met this cheeky lad a few years ago, he was all but living on the streets of Nairobi. He was about twelve years old. Now and again I would visit his old grandmother, Kiboko, and now and again Kasuki would visit his old grandmother, so that was how we met.

Kiboko is a very old lady who lives in a hovel of thrown-out packing materials along the Nairobi River. She is old and somewhat eccentric, but there is still a sparkle in her eyes when her grandson turns up to visit her.

She took Kasuki and his brother Mudei into her house when their mother died. For years she looked after the children. Kasuki wasn't even five when his mother died. Kiboko cared for them. True, they didn't get all that much to eat, and the diet was not exactly what a child should have, but the old lady compensated for the lack of calories by telling beautiful stories about the giraffe, the hyena, the elephant and the rabbit. For years Kasuki thrived on these, but as he grew older he started to find his grandmother a bit childish. Then he began hanging around with other small boys who also had no chance of going to school. They lived in the streets: the so-called parkingboys. Kasuki had to learn a lot, and he picked up things quickly. He learned to smoke *banghi* (pot) and how to sniff petrol and get high on it. He learned to park cars and to grab what he could in the process. In short, he learned to survive in the jungle of the big city, Nairobi. It is a rough and tough life. Kasuki became a hard, devilish little fellow, but he never lost his heart. He would never spend his entire take on sex films, drugs and coca-cola, but always saved something for his old granny. Once he even stole a piece of meat for her, and stealing meat is a hazardous business.

It was quite some time before I was able to convince Kasuki that he could have a better future if he left the street and went to one of the informal schools run by Undugu. These are special schools for boys and girls who cannot go to the ordinary primary (elementary) school for various economic and social reasons. Many of the pupils are former parkingboys, and others would have soon become parkingboys if they had not been in these schools. Kasuki and I talked about it several times and I proposed that we should go together to have a look. The boy agreed to go along with this, not because he was seriously interested in my proposal, but because he wanted to have a ride in a car with a European driver! In the school, however, he met some of his former street buddies and they seemed happy enough, so Kasuki said he was willing to give it a try.

I must admit, in the beginning he did not try very hard. He would come for a few days and show some interest in reading and writing, but then he would slope off back to the streets for days on end. After all, he had to make a living, and besides, school life was a bit tame compared with the excitement of the streets.

The headmistress was very understanding when I visited the school. She would say, "That son of yours, Kasuki, has disappeared again."

I would go and look around near the city market and when I found him we would talk some more. Everything would be settled and Kasuki would agree to let me drive him back to school; imagining himself the son of a rich man. "Ah, you have brought your son again," Miss Wamboyi would say jokingly, and she would send him back to his group. But a few weeks later it would be the same old story.

Once I tried to give him a good telling off. It was about time that he made a serious effort and he had to choose the school or the street—he couldn't have both. His street life would end in prison. But my whole sermon seemed to fall flat. Kasuki just eyed me up and down, not at all impressed. In any case, who am I to tell Kasuki about life? On the streets the boys endure more hardship in a month than many of us do in a lifetime.

Somehow he gradually got involved in this school business. His reading and writing are nothing to shout about; others with whom he started are now in more advanced groups. But luckily there are other important subjects at school—like drama. When Kasuki acted the old drunk, everybody doubled up with laughter. He is mechanically-minded, too; removing and replacing a Volkswagen headlight takes Kasuki only a few minutes. Where do you get that kind of service in a garage these days? Then again, there is the distinct possibility that Kasuki might palm the new bulb and pocket it in the process. Pilfering is a bad habit formed in the streets.

Eventually Kasuki decided that after finishing school he wanted to become a mechanic. Things started to look up for him.

But then, last year, he had to face a new reality. His grandmother became increasingly senile. She couldn't look after Kasuki and Mudei any longer. She herself had to be looked after by the neighbours. It was decided that the two boys would have to go back to their father who lived somewhere in Mathare Valley. They were not consulted about it. They understood that they did have a father somewhere, but he had hardly ever visited them. All said and done, there really wasn't much choice, so they went.

That dad of his has been one big disappointment as far as Kasuki is concerned. He has no job and he is continually drunk. Kasuki gets more beatings from him than food, but that is not all. Mathare Valley is a lot farther from his school. Now and again Kasuki travels part of the journey, hanging onto a bus. That is dangerous, and some time ago Kasuki badly hurt his foot when he fell off. The next day he came to see me. He was limping and he asked for money for the bus fare to go to school. After all, wasn't I the one who wanted him to go to school? He had a point there and he exploited it very well.

But then, asking for money often makes enemies out of friends. In the end I gave him the bus fare, after making him promise that it would be the last time he asked for money. Kasuki promised solemnly.

He still goes and visits his grandmother occasionally, but she is deteriorating fast. Kasuki finds that he hasn't got much of a grandmother any more. But one of the teachers tells me that there is no storyteller like Kasuki in the whole school. I am glad to hear that something of Kiboko lives on in Kasuki.

Not so long ago Kasuki came to see me again. He looked miserable. His father had beaten him up, but Kasuki can stand a beating. His brother had received a new pair of secondhand trousers but Kasuki hadn't got anything. He was dressed in rags, but he could put up with that too. No, the worst thing was that his father had told him that he wasn't his father, and that his mother had been a whore and he didn't want anything to do with Kasuki any more. The tale was as miserable as Kasuki looked. I didn't know what to say, but I did have some secondhand clothing. I went to look for a pair of trousers. They fit, more or less, and he cheered up a little. But he obviously had not come for a pair of trousers.

Kasuki looked at me and went on, "People call you 'father' but you have no children. Teacher Wamboyi calls me your son. Now my father has thrown me out. Can't you be my father?"

That was quite a request and I must admit that for a moment I was tempted to say Yes. But then this was not such a simple matter. I think that a father should be more experienced in life than his son, and I know Kasuki had gone through a lot. Moreover, he had been let down so often; it would be bad if he were to be left in the lurch again by me. I don't think I would really qualify to be a father to Kasuki. We talked for a long time and it wasn't easy. In the end we came to a compromise. I couldn't be a father to him, but I would try to be his friend. That is at least something in life, having a friend, especially when one is unlucky with relatives. He accepts this. "Will you give me the bus fare to go to school tomorrow?" he asked. Damn it, how can you refuse such a simple request from a friend? He traveled by bus the next day, needless to say!

By staying always in the same place, one gets lice. —Kikuyu proverb

UNDUGU BEAT

With a nearly empty bag carelessly slung across his shoulder, his guitar between his legs, an American baseball cap sideways on his head, Gitau stands at the bar drinking a beer. He is just practising being nonchalant now that he is flying to Germany in an hour's time. He is one of the nine 'stars' who constitute the 'famous' group Undugu Beat, which is going to conquer Germany. It is quite a jump from the stinking Mathare Valley, the biggest slum of Nairobi, to Cologne and German television. Gitau looks at Father Grol who, with a full bag over his shoulder, is standing in the airport lounge talking enthusiastically to everyone, smoking one cigarette after another. Gitau is wondering what they have let themselves in for; he knows that when you move with this priest, anything can happen.

Years ago, Father Arnold Grol began this band. Strictly speaking, he was not really the founder because he did not have the faintest idea what he was starting when he gave a few guitars to some boys in Mathare Valley. Things just happened. The boys started playing and they played well. A German journalist saw them and decided there was some real talent amongst them. He wrote about them and Germany gave a lot of money for electrical instruments for these boys. Undugu Beat began to look like a real band, although at times they remain more like a troop of bandits!

They play in The Goats, a club for young people in Mathare, and they also play at parties in embassies. For such occasions they have even learned to play softly. The band has cut an L.P., of which they are very proud. But they are more proud of the fact that they have been invited to play for the German television. This evening they are flying there and Father Grol is going along with them.

There has been a lot of preparation. Yesterday we spent most of the day together taking care of the last-minute details. I tried to explain a little about what to expect in far distant Germany. But that was as difficult as explaining to people in London or Los Angeles what life is like in the slums of Nairobi.

The members of the band really do want to make the best of this trip, but they know they have one or two problems. Drinking is one of them. Mwangi is 'tipsy' already, and that makes him sad. He only livens up when he is absolutely drunk. We discuss these matters—a long and tedious talk. We can't have this in Germany; it will be more of a problem than it was on the occasion when they got drunk at an embassy party. At last they decide that Gatuguta, the leader of the band, will see to it that there is no drinking before a show. Gatuguta suggests that Nicodemus, his drinking buddy, will assist him there. It is a chancy arrangement but we have to take a some risks.

Rosemary, the singer of the band, and the only member who never drinks, gets the impossible task of keeping an eye on everybody when they have a drink or two after a show. They really don't want to make a drunken mess of it. They talk about unity, about not quarreling and wonder who will be the most popular amongst them; they all feel as if they are little 'big stars,' but they realize that they cannot make it to the top on their own.

Flora, who has a few children, is a bit more practical. She talks about buying clothes, or rather about acquiring them, as well as other nice things. They hope to receive lots of presents and gifts, but they decide now to share what they get because otherwise they foresee quarrels. Gitau, who seems to have more self-confidence, is asked to look after the everyday events of the group, and he is asked to mediate any disputes there may be.

Kiarie, the young acrobat, is another problem. For years he wandered about with a group of street musicians. At present he goes to school, and at the same time, he is a member of Undugu Beat. In this way he can earn some money for himself and his grandmother. He is only eleven years old and somebody will have to look after him. Flora and Mwangi are asked to be surrogate mother and father to Kiarie, who has been an orphan for years.

Father Grol also attends our meeting. Finances are discussed. Michael, who wants to be called 'Mike' during the trip, is of the opinion that Undugu ought to pay them well. There is silence... Of course everybody would like to get a lot of money, but they want to be reasonable about it. Njenga, one of the guitarists, asked Mike where he would be without Undugu. Doesn't Undugu (Brotherhood) also mean sharing together, and sharing with the many brothers who are not going to Germany? I am pleased that it's one of the band who says this and not Father Grol or myself. Mike gives in with a shrug; it was worth trying anyway.

Late that evening we have a beer in one of the many day-and-night clubs in Eastleigh. They fancy themselves as stars. Tomorrow they are going to Germany, but Gatuguta says, "I spreak gar nichts German."

We had arranged to meet this evening at seven o'clock. At half past seven the first three arrive, Mike, Flora, and Rosemary. Mike, seeing that he is the first, wants to get some tea at the Cloud Nine kiosk just around the corner. The girls advise me to go along because they are afraid that Mike might disappear into the bar to steady his nerves. All four of us go to the kiosk for some tea.

When we return, the others are arriving. Njenga is quite far gone: reeking of chang'aa. He leans on my shoulder whilst he tries to explain to me, "That plane is very big and flies very high and when it stops, you know, crash, bang, wallop, gone is Njenga, gone Undugu Beat, gone Germany."

I try to assure him that there is nothing to worry about; a plane is safer than the matatu in which he travels every day, safer than a bus. He looks at me, not quite believing me, and in the end, he says, "Ah, Matthew, you can't know this. You are not going to Cologne tonight." And then after a short silence, "Can't we take the bus?"

Kiarie, carrying his new bag, appears confident but a little nervous too when he finally arrives at Father Grol's room. It is a relief that he has arrived. One of his uncles tried to kidnap him this morning in the hope of getting some money out of Father Grol.

We all go together to the Brilliant Hotel where you can eat a lot of ugali (maize porridge) for a little money. The band often eats here. It will be a few weeks before they can eat ugali again. We have to wait, so they take out their guitars. Together they sing, 'Silent Night, Holy Night' in German, which they have learned for the occasion. It sounds dull. It is clearly not their own choice. Then, talking and encouraging each other, they begin to sing and live their own songs, *I Am a Child of Ten Shillings*.[†] Nicodemus gets up and half-drunk stumbles over a chair. But then he sings and acts with his whole body. Tables are shifted and young Kiarie tumbles and rolls over the floor, doing his acrobatic stunts. The people at the bar are the audience and they start applauding. The band, dancing and singing, gives away a free show just like that. When they sit down again, even Njenga smiles and says, "A pity that you can't see us next Sunday on TV; then we will be even better."

When we arrive at the airport we discover that, in all the excitement, little Kiarie left his bag in Father Grol's room. I drive back to Eastleigh with him to collect it. As we pass Mathare Valley, Kiarie asks if we could call at his grandmother's house for a few minutes, just to say goodbye to her. When I explain that we have no time for that, he accepts. He tells me that he has promised the old woman a present from Germany and she was very happy about that.

Now they have to board the plane; they say goodbye to us and we wish them good luck. I shake hands with Flora and she says, "I will bring a present for you, even if it is something small." Maybe I am becoming a little bit of an old woman, as I too feel happy about that promise!

[†] 'I am the child of a prostitute.'

A cow must graze where she is tied. —Proverb from Sierra Leone

GRACE

I was on the point of leaving Mathare Valley for the day when Grace stopped me. It can be very tiresome when all kinds of people try to get something from you. When you talk about school sponsorships, everybody seems to become a lot poorer. People can drain you. I was tired, but Grace insisted that she had to see me; no, not here, but in her house.

Often it is more tiring to disagree than to agree, so I went along with Grace to her hut where she lives with a few of her sisters. This shack is not as dirty and dark as most of the others. There are some posters on the walls, which do something towards brightening up the place. But Grace herself looks very gloomy. She wants to talk about that kid of hers. The child is nearly two years old. Grace happened to get pregnant when she was in the secondary school, so she was expelled, and gone was her chance of getting a job. The father of the child didn't want to know her any more. "Anyway, that is how men are," says Grace.

Men have spoiled her life. She hates them with a vengeance, as is the case with many prostitutes. Her life had gone down the drain, she thought. "But forget it, it's not your worry, Matthew, that would be a waste of time."

But that kid of hers; *I* would have to find a home for that child. She couldn't stand it any longer. Just imagine, having to go streetwalking just to look after a child! The child was only a big burden. I, as a do-gooder, could take it along. Grace wasn't very gracious about all this. She was a handsome young woman at one time, but now she looked ugly, and cared nothing for herself or others.

It was clear that she wasn't interested in any pious platitudes. I told her that I had no intention of picking up what she threw away, and that she could bloody well make a new start. The child didn't need a home; it needed her as a mother. Her life was by no means spoiled, unless she herself went on to spoil it. I must say, I gave her quite a sermon. Grace looked at me as if to say, "To hell with you," and I felt I was being classified with all the other men who couldn't be relied upon.

A few weeks later we wanted to start a youth club in that area. I went back to Grace and asked her to give the girls a hand; after all, she had spent a few years at secondary school.

"Hmm, they don't want me," she answered, "and you refused to look for a home for my child." I ignored that last remark and explained that the other girls would appreciate her help.

She did it. She practised with the girls and they formed a good netball team. They won the first two matches, but during the third match they had a referee who was partial. I suppose every referee is biased, but this one showed it. He was clearly against Grace's team. She ran up to him, snatched his whistle and threw it away. Of course, the referee was a man; they were like that, but she wasn't prepared to stand for it any longer. Furious, she wasn't going to play any more with a referee like that.

Without knowing or intending it, Grace became the leader of the girls and they went on practising and playing. When a few new teachers were needed in our informal school, I advised Grace to go for the interview.

"You will see, they will only take men. They will certainly not accept me because I have a child, or have you finally decided to find a home for that kid?"

"Grace, I won't even think about it. I have seen how happy your mother is with her grandchild. It is a great pity that you yourself aren't happy with the child," I told her.

The panel which interviewed her thought more of her than she did of herself. She certainly knew what children in the slums of Nairobi had to go through. To her own astonishment she got the job.

She started teaching boys and girls from the slums who had missed their chance to go to government primary school. For months Grace was doing well and her gloomy face was transformed. But then one evening she called on me and she was really miserable. "Now I am in for it. I had a real quarrel with the headmistress. The headmistress wanted to send a girl away from school. It was unfair. We had a big quarrel and I think I am going to be sacked."

Suddenly her life wasn't worth a penny any more and she felt the whole world was against her.

"Grace can be fierce, but she fights for her children. She will become a very good teacher," the headmistress told me when I asked her what had happened. There was no question of her being sacked, but Grace had walked away in anger.

Perhaps I should have told Grace that the headmistress had a good opinion of her, but instead I simply told her that she would not be sacked. I also asked her how she could fight for the children of others, whilst she wanted to give her own child away.

Grace didn't think that was a fair question and she didn't answer.

She continued teaching and she did a good job. She often ate her school lunch with Chegge. Chegge is a teacher himself. He is a very positive thinker, and many of the pupils confide in him. He is father, mother, social worker and educator rolled into one. The children had told him that Grace was a good person and he knew they told the truth.

Last year there was an interview for the teacher training college. Grace was advised to attend. Surprised, but without much hope, she went along. It would be six weeks before they heard the results, but after two weeks Grace decided that she didn't have a chance. On the other hand, Chegge, kept telling her that she had a very good chance. But according to Grace, Chegge was naive. That naive Chegge had even told her that he loved her. Grace had been disappointed; she had just started to think that Chegge was one of the few good men around. But Grace knew that when men began talking like that, they only wanted to go to bed with you. Marriage was out of the question as far as she was concerned. She had that child and she didn't have a good job, unless the teacher training course... But Grace wouldn't think about that. She had no chance.

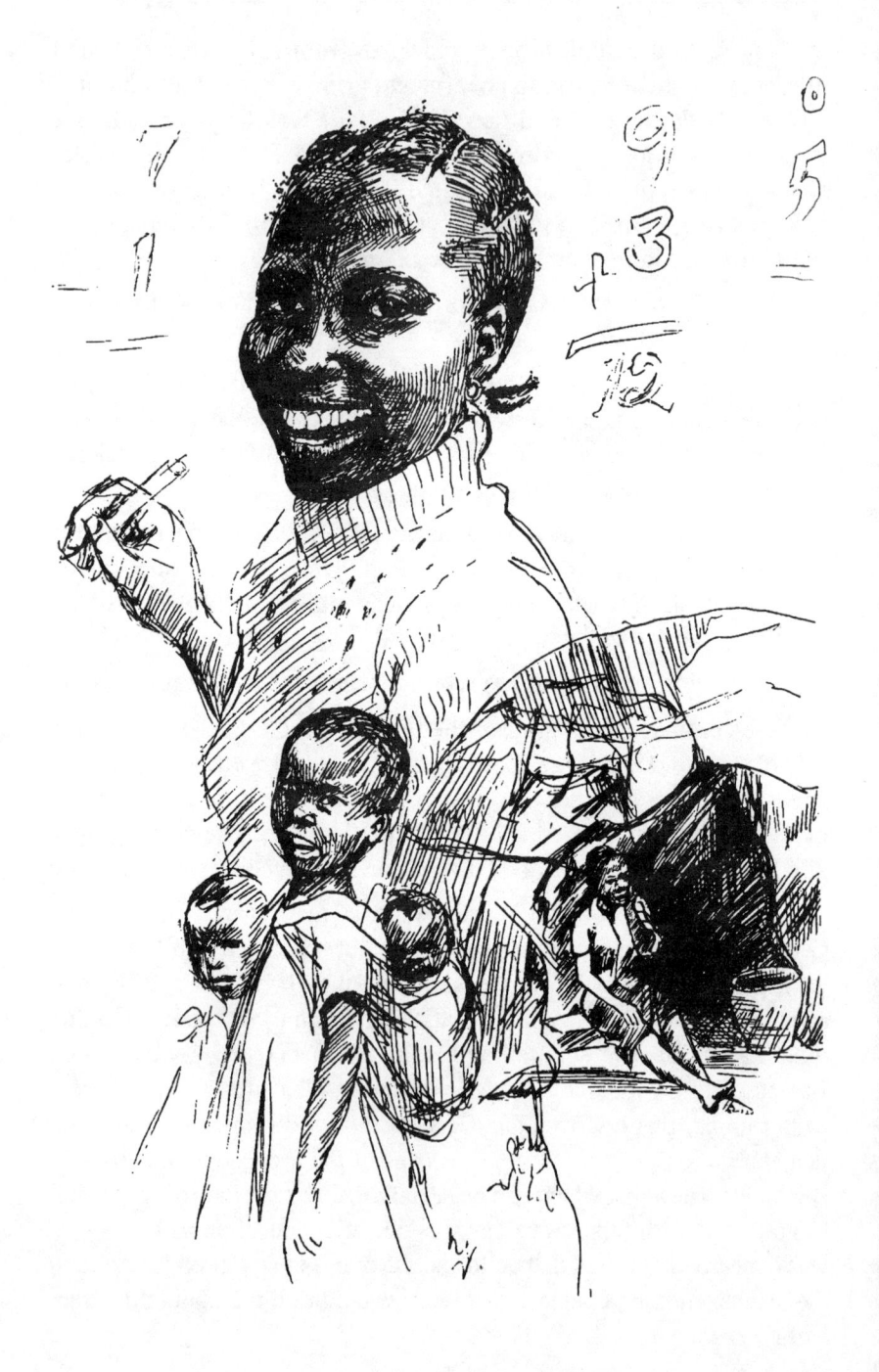

Now Grace is in a teacher training college and occasionally I receive greetings from her via Chegge. She writes to him quite often. A few weeks ago she was here, on her first holidays. She came to greet me and her little boy was with her.

"He hasn't seen me for months, but he only wants to be with me," she says happily. He plays around on her lap and she hugs him.

Grace is on her way to see Chegge. I have to go that way too and I offer her a lift in the car. On the way, she tells me that after she has completed her studies, Chegge is going to marry her. Chegge also thinks that they should baptize "their" child, this little boy who is trying to pull her hair. No more mention of another home for him.

Grace looks young again and full of joy. This whole scene, mother and child, Grace in love, makes me quite happy. Maybe love is contagious.

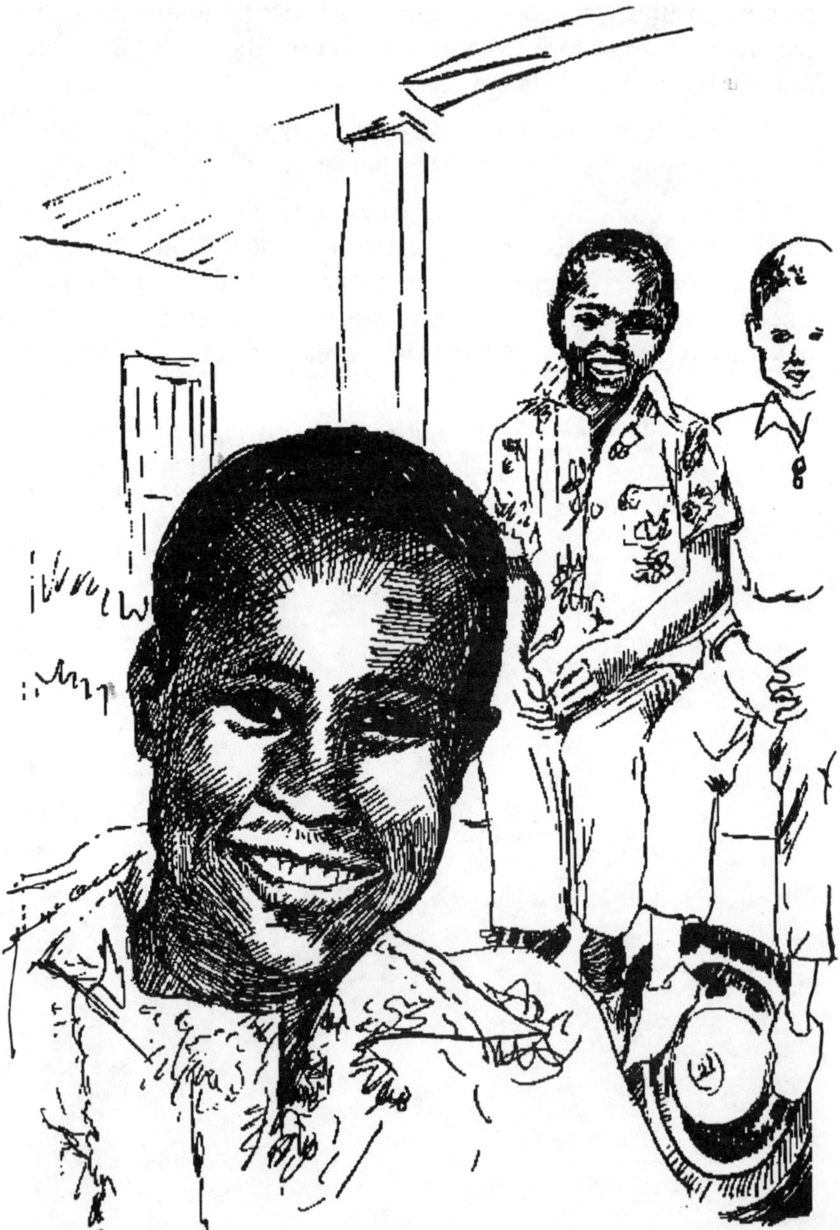

*Rain beats a leopard's skin
but it does not wash out the spots.* —ASHANTI PROVERB

PARKINGBOY

Magugu is wearing the big cap of the night watchman at the Undugu Centre. The night watchman is also on duty during the day, but he has taken a break. Parkingboy Magugu is his usual standby when he goes for a cup of tea or when he suddenly has to go and visit a friend. The big cap nearly falls over the boy's eyes as he chases a few tearaway kids with his stick. He really tries to hit them, but he has to drag his polio leg along and they easily escape. They then have a good laugh at the standby watchman from a safe distance. Magugu is blindingly angry with them.

Then he sees me and the small, furious devil becomes a friendly little boy under an outsize cap. Smiling all over his face, he opens the gate for me. He drags his leg a bit more and without my asking him, assures me that he will watch my car. He informs me that some of those boys cannot be trusted. He is a real charmer, but he definitely discriminates against his own race.

Magugu knows his clients and he has his own particular psychological approach. He has not studied psychology from a book, but his experience in the streets of Nairobi has taught him how to handle people. He knows which approach pays: the best way to handle Europeans—be friendly, mildly obliging, put on a humble look. If it doesn't work, try a cheeky smile, that is often successful. Those Europeans are the most generous clients for the parkingboys, especially when they have expensive goods in their cars, then they give an extra tip in the hope that you guard their car instead of robbing it. Yes, the Europeans are good customers. Magugu prefers them to the Asians most days of the week, except

Fridays, of course. This is the day that many Asians give alms to the poor, so on Fridays Magugu makes the most of his poverty. He exaggerates dragging his polio leg and he puts on his hungry and pitiful look and hangs around the temples. In that way he helps the Asians to fulfill their religious duty. On other days they are not very generous towards parkingboys. He knows where he stands with them.

African men are more complicated, unpredictable. At times they can be very stern and don't give you even a *ndururu*[†] but at other times they might give you a lift and buy you a meal of tea and bread at a kiosk. A cup of tea and a few slices of bread is a pretty good meal for a parkingboy. But it is a bit awkward when the offer is made at peak hours. Anyway, like most parkingboys, Magugu prefers cash. He prefers African men to African women drivers. He despises the latter. African women behind the steering wheel— he wouldn't bother to find a parking place for them. They don't give you anything except the useless advice that you should go back to your mother. They irritate him immensely, because the last thing he wants to do is go back to that mother of his in the dark shop in Loitokitok.

That is where he was born, Loitokitok. A hole of a place, if you ask Magugu. The realization came over him when his mother brought him to Nairobi to see whether the doctors here could improve his polio leg. That was his first contact with the city and he definitely liked it. The doctors gave him a calliper for his leg, but he considered it more of a nuisance than a help. However, the city of Nairobi had made a deep impression on six-year-old Magugu. He agreed with the tourist brochures that it was the most beautiful city in the world. He wanted to go back there and get away from the dreary life in his mother's small shop where the customers got more attention than he did.

Every day a few ramshackle buses travel from Loitokitok to Nairobi, a journey of more than 200 kilometers. The first time Magugu decided to go as a stowaway, he was about seven years old. Of course he was discovered, but when the bus conductor noticed him, they were already in the Maasai plains, and it is hard

---

[†] Ndururu: a five cent piece, the smallest coin in Kenya.

to dump a small boy out there in the middle of the wild animals. You would have to be a beast yourself to do such a thing. Moreover, Magugu looked very apologetic and the conductor somehow liked him. In Nairobi, the little boy managed to slip away from the conductor, who would have taken him back home. Later on, Magugu's mother had such a terrific row with the conductor that he no longer likes that little boy.

Magugu was inexperienced in the city life, and inexperienced boys get picked up by the police. Soon he was back in Loitokitok, rehabilitated by the Juvenile Court. Again that dreary life, he didn't fancy it at all. He wanted to get back to Nairobi, but the conductor wouldn't give him another chance. There was another bus, on which he was not known to the conductor, so one morning the small boy turned up as a passenger. He had money for a ticket and a little more besides. He seemed to know exactly where he was going, and there was no reason to refuse him. Half an hour later Magugu's mother discovered that the cashbox in the shop was empty.

In Nairobi, Magugu was more careful than the first time, and managed to avoid being caught. He showed initiative by joining a gang of other boys and learned fast. Soon he found out that he did not have to spend the nights in a cold doorway or in a plastic bag at the city market. He found a better place to settle down—on the gratings of the kitchen of the New Stanley Hotel. The warm air from the kitchen was as good as a blanket. Another advantage was that he caught the late customers from the hotel or the cinemas, and it was here that he learned how to tackle the different races of Nairobi. It looked like Magugu was set up for life, but his mother had informed the police, and in the end his polio leg betrayed him and the police picked him up once more.

Back again to Loitokitok. He couldn't understand why his mother had been looking for him; now that she had found him all she did was scold him. He could not stand it for long. He was too much of a townsman to live in such a provincial hole. The buses to Nairobi wouldn't take him any more. However, Loitokitok is at the border of Tanzania, and buses were going in that direction as well. So Magugu decided to emigrate to another country.

One afternoon he stepped off the bus in the town of Moshi. Compared with Nairobi, Moshi is only a small town, and it isn't much of a town for parkingboys. Magugu was going to have to do some pioneering. There were not so many cars, and very few Europeans and Asians, but there was plenty of parking space. The few street kids who were there had no training at all; they didn't seem to know that parkingboys were there to be given money! A few were trained by Magugu personally, but they were slow learners, and he had no proper gang to assist him. No, Moshi was not a happy hunting ground, especially when a policeman caught the boy. He quickly admitted that he was a Kenyan from Loitokitok and was repatriated at the cost of the Tanzanian government.

Magugu kept dreaming about Nairobi, especially when his mother wanted to use him as an errand boy. At heart he is a capitalist and he stands for free enterprise. But he could not get away. He was being watched at the bus station; he felt like a rat in a trap. In the end he tried another adventure. He made a long detour and went in the opposite direction, all the way to Mombasa. He begged from the tourists and he lived soberly, for he had to save for the journey to Nairobi. He would leave his savings with a lady at a kiosk.

And so a few years ago he finally arrived in Nairobi to join his pals, a gang of parkingboys. He learned a few new techniques. Parking is a real problem in the city, especially when you have to keep going back to feed the meter. Magugu would do that for you. You could leave a shilling with him and he would promise to keep the parking meter full. But then he would pocket the money and put an extra half hour on your meter by using the plastic refill of a ballpoint pen. This is a special technique known only to 'insiders' and Magugu is an insider. He often earned more than an unskilled labourer, but then you really can't call Magugu unskilled. He also became something of a thief.

He did not give up all of this when he finally decided to join Undugu. Maybe in the beginning he saw it as an easy way to make a living. He would stay for a few weeks; he would be nice to everybody and he was very well behaved. People began to trust him and then he would choose his opportunity. Something would go missing and Magugu usually went missing too. A few days later Father Grol would meet him again on the street. Once he even had the cheek to steal a white baby from a stroller in front of a shop and offer it for sale to passersby. We had to laugh about it, but the mother didn't think it was at all funny.

Now he lives a little more ordered life in one of the homes for parkingboys near Mathare Valley. He goes to school, not every day of course, but pretty regularly. As far as some of the teachers are concerned, he could stay away more often. Very often Magugu means trouble. A few weeks ago, all the padlocks of the teachers' cupboards went missing. By the time it was discovered, Magugu had sold them to people in Mathare Valley at knock-down prices. The teachers, the social worker, the house father, everybody was furious with him. Magugu couldn't stand that people should be angry with him; they hadn't even proved that he had done it.

He was still denying his crime when he disappeared again. His luck held in that there was a big conference in the city. With the great number of visitors, it was a heyday for the parkingboys. He stayed away from Undugu long enough for everybody to cool down. Then he came back with the pitiful story that he had been picked up by the police and that he had been in the police station for days. Nobody really believed him, but at the same time it could have been true. He got off lightly again.

It is not an easy job to educate Magugu. Maybe the watchman's approach is as good as any. Magugu guards the gate for him. One way of stopping a poacher is to make him the gamekeeper, or so they say...

What God preserves for the poor doesn't get spoiled.—Kikuyu proverb

GOD WILL LOOK AFTER EVERYTHING

In order to enter her home you have to be humble and bend your head very low because the doorway is also very low. Her shack has been built against the slope of Mathare Valley. We crawl in; it is an awful, dark hole. But a Kenya proverb says, 'Despise not the hut before you know who sleeps there.' Helen Mumbi isn't sleeping at the moment and she warmly welcomes Sister Piedad and I. Helen is very hospitable and visitors are always welcome.

She is quite a woman, so stocky and well-built that a dock worker would be proud if he had arms like hers. On a charcoal stove she is brewing tea mixed with a lot of milk. At the same time she is busy sewing a patchwork cover. She invites us to sit down as she moves towards the doorway to sell a tin of charcoal. Part of her living is made in this way. She inquires after my health, and gives Piedad the latest news about their mutual friends. She scolds us in a friendly way for having stayed away too long. At the same time she gives a brief sermon to an old woman who is lying on her bed. "Your leg will get better soon. God will see to that. You must give him time; just pray, but don't tell him what to do. He knows what he is going to do, but he will do it his own way and in his own time. And if you don't believe me, ask Mathew. He is a priest."

I don't like to disagree with Helen, certainly when she is talking about her friend, God, who helped her out so often. I inquire who this woman is—another relative of hers? No, it is a woman from the neighbourhood; she can hardly walk. Helen has to be at home for her charcoal trade, so she is able to look after the neighbour during the day. "If one can help, one should help." It is as simple as that for Helen. *"Kusaidia ni kuwekesha akeba,"* she says—friendly assistance is like an investment.

Victoria, a small girl of about three, walks in and wants to sit on Helen's lap. She is very welcome to do so, but first Victoria has to shake hands with the visitors. This child is Helen's pride and joy, and she spends a lot of time with her, showing her affection and love. So many children receive very little affection here in Mathare Valley; the mothers don't seem to find the time. Fortunately, Helen can do many things at the same time.

Again Helen tells the old woman to trust in God; didn't God give her Victoria? And would she have expected that to happen at that time and in that place? Helen certainly has tremendous confidence in God, but it wasn't always like that.

Helen came with her parents to Mathare Valley when she was still a child, and when the place wasn't as crowded as it is today. Growing up here was hard: she knew poverty and she was drenched with the rough life of Mathare Valley. She seemed doomed to end up in the gutter like so many around her. Her only treasure was her three children. She no longer knows who the fathers were because at that time she was frequently drunk. She tells Piedad that she didn't drink weak beer like the Europeans; no, she drank the real stuff, the chang'aa that keeps burning in your stomach.

Helen talks openly about her past. She isn't ashamed of it. Her sister managed to get out of Mathare and looked for a better life in Uganda. Helen merely continued to exist in Mathare and her eldest daughter moved in with a man and left the house. Even when she was drunk, Helen loved her youngest daughter very much indeed. This daughter became sick and Helen didn't know what sickness she had. Some people said it was malaria of the brain. One evening the young girl went to the toilet across the road and she didn't come back. When others went to look for her they found her dead; she had died in the toilet.

Helen was heartbroken. Her most beloved child had died and in a toilet, of all places. It happened about four years ago. She vaguely remembers the funeral. Somebody had said, "God who takes life away from us can also return it to us." It was then that Helen started to pray. Sometimes she was half-drunk, but frequently she was very sober. Maybe she wasn't too old yet to have another child.

One evening Helen went to the toilet; she went together with two other women, which is safer in the evening. Drunken men don't bother you then. Whilst they were in the toilet they heard a baby crying. Perhaps there was a woman with the baby in one of the cubicles. However, when they went to leave, the baby was still crying. A good mother shouldn't let her baby cry. The women called out, "Who is there?" Nobody answered. They listened and then went to have a look. In one of the cubicles they found a new-born baby, wrapped up in a newspaper.

That night the baby stayed with Helen. Next morning they reported it to the police, but the police aren't so good at caring for new-born babies. A report was filed, and when the women asked whether they could keep the baby, the police said that they could if the mother didn't turn up. They knew that the mother wouldn't appear. Mothers who leave babies in toilets usually don't report to the police. Helen and her friend both wanted to have the baby, but they didn't discuss it too much. After all, Helen thought this was a clear case which didn't need much discussion. The baby had stayed with *her* during the night, not only that—hadn't her own daughter died in those very same toilets? Wasn't this baby the obvious answer to all her prayers of the last few months? The baby stayed with Helen, but it was very sick with some kind of skin disease. Helen looked after the child and went to several doctors. Sister Piedad was helpful and advised her now and again. The child survived though Helen didn't give much credit to the doctors. She thanked God who had given her this child, who had shown that he cared for her. He had cured her child.

She wanted the baby to be baptized, but in such matters the life of the parents plays a role too. Helen's life was not exactly that of an exemplary Christian. Yes, she herself had been baptized and she had some friends who were Christians, but that was as far as it went.

"God loves you, but do you love him?" somebody asked her. "What kind of life are you going to give this child?"

Helen pondered that question. Certainly it was a rough life she led, but how could she earn a living without the chang'aa trade? God had helped before and so she discussed the entire matter with him. If she gave up the whole world of drinking and prostitution, then God would have to help her in some other business. It turned out that her new charcoal business went well, and she was able to earn some other money with the patchwork she was doing. Her child was baptized Victoria.

Her sister in Uganda kept writing to say that she was in trouble. Her husband had abandoned her and her four children. Somebody had to help. Helen borrowed some money and she took the bus to Uganda, a place where hardly anybody dared venture at the time. She bribed her way across the border, found her sister and brought her back to Mathare Valley. Her sister was an alcoholic. Helen added a small room to her shack and she looked after her sister and the children. She worked day and night; that was as much as she could do. Her friend, God, whom Helen talks about all the time, would have to see to the rest. Nobody went to bed feeling hungry, Helen assures us.

"Do you still believe he won't help you?" she asks the old woman on her bed. "He helped me and I certainly wasn't a good woman. I know he is going to help you."

Helen became an active member of a small Christian community in her neighbourhood. She is a witness to her faith by the life she leads, and wherever she goes Victoria goes too. She is her 'show baby.' For some time people called the child the *choo baby,* which means toilet baby, but one day Helen made it quite clear that something would happen to the next person who dared to mention that nickname again. People knew that Helen didn't make idle threats; now her child is called Victoria by everybody.

As I listen to Helen and watch as she does three things at once, she reminds me of the strong woman in the Book of Proverbs (31:17). She is energetic, a hard worker and watches for bargains. She works far into the night. —And that is exactly what Helen does. A strong woman, but who will find her? It isn't clear whether Kago found her or whether she found Kago. Kago is a decent guy.

He even has a small job. But it is Helen who runs the home, with God's help, of course.

Helen took Kago to the local Christian community and explained to the people there that this Kago was now her husband. It is perhaps a pity that this statement made in front of the community isn't recognized as a church marriage. But marriage in church is a complicated matter and it will take time. I have the impression that Helen is more understanding towards the Church than the official Church is towards Helen.

She offers us a second cup of her dreadfully sweet tea; she is extremely generous with sugar. Once again she assures us that God is always there to help her and that he will look after everything. Whilst I drink her tea, I think of the African saying: *What God preserves for the poor doesn't become spoiled.*

A bad son gives a bad name to his mother. —IVORY COAST PROVERB

ATTEMPTED MURDER

Sina Makosa—I don't make mistakes, is painted on the side of the matatu that rushes to overtake me. The road is too narrow and he leans on his horn, forcing me off the road. I have to slam on my brakes to prevent the car from ending up in the ditch. Badly shaken, I curse that matatu driver as I slide to a halt on the side of the road.

Some people who saw what happened help me to curse the driver, others just laugh; they think it is a good joke. Then all of a sudden there stands Wangare. She has a big bandage around her head, and even though she is a bit tipsy she saw what happened.

She does not laugh, but enthusiastically helps me to curse this driver who didn't even bother to stop. She knows these drivers. As a street-sweeper in Nairobi she frequently has to dodge these lethal matatus. I am only listening to her with half an ear as my shock slowly wears off. Then I hear her say, "Matatu drivers are murderers, just like my son."

What? Her son a murderer? I know her children, the eldest is a parkingboy, about twelve years old. What on earth is she talking about? Wangare grabs her son Kiarie from behind the car, and, holding him by his shirt, shoves him in front of me as if bringing the accused into court.

This boy threw a stone at her head, his very own mother, just imagine. "Attempted murder," Wangare calls it. Now she is going to take him to the police; they will have to send him to a remand home. "There they will teach him a job, this good-for-nothing," Wangare says angrily. Kiarie obviously couldn't care less. He looks at his mother with contempt. He doesn't seem to be at all sorry.

Before Wangare makes a big scene here in the middle of the street, I ask them both to get into the car. "Up to the police station," she orders. Kiarie sits in the back as if he has nothing at all to do with this.

I don't think a police station is the place for small boys and so I suggest that I drive them home instead. Wangare protests and she shows me the scratch under her big bandage and starts talking again about attempted murder.

"Moreover, he will learn a job in the remand home," she says. I assure her that the police can't send all the streetboys to remand homes; there are too many streetboys and too few homes.

"They may cane him a few times," I say, "or perhaps they will arrest you for being drunk."

She looks at me as if to say, "It isn't nice of you to bring that up."

It puts her in a milder mood. She isn't very much in favour of this caning either. Ten strokes of the cane is a lot for a boy of twelve years. But a remand home would be good; she has heard that the boys learn a job there and they also get some discipline. I explain that I have my doubts about the educational value of these remand centres. In the meantime, I am not driving in the direction of the police station, but we are going to Igloo Village, along the Nairobi River where Wangare lives.

Kiarie sits almost proudly in the back seat. He feels that he is winning and that once again he has escaped the police. If he looked a little more repentant, I might be able to win over his mother. I give him a bit of a dressing down about throwing stones at his mother, but he just looks at me as if to say, "You don't know what you are talking about. You just don't know my mother!"

When I stop my car in the village he jumps out and challenges people with a look that says, "Dare touch me and I'll throw a stone at you!" Wangare tries to have her say once more to the people standing around. They listen in silence; it's no use arguing with a woman who is drunk.

Later, one of the neighbours tells me that it is all the fault of Wangare's husband. " I didn't know that Wangare had a husband," I say.

"Well, no, he's not really a husband anymore; he left her years ago."

He didn't leave because Wangare was a bad woman or something like that; in that case he could still have beaten her. No, the poverty just became too much for him. No job, no home, a wife and four kids, he just couldn't cope with it. One has to be very strong to be able to bear all that, and often only a woman is strong enough.

However, the husband had been here this afternoon to visit Wangare. They drank together and they talked about the children. When he heard that Kiarie was a parkingboy, the father had been very disappointed. His eldest son, his hope, a petty thief. It was a big blow to him. He accused Wangare of driving the boy onto the streets. She should have cared better for him. She had surely neglected him; it was her fault.

Wangare, perhaps feeling a little guilty, had become angry. This was bloody man's talk. How could she keep an eye on Kiarie? From eight to five she swept the streets, and in that way she was able at least to feed the children. And he, what did *he* do for the children? Nothing at all. Tempers flared: how could he help? It wasn't his fault that there were no jobs in Nairobi. He didn't want his son to be a failure as he felt himself to be. In the end, he had said that he wanted to take his son along with him. Then the real quarrel started.

First he had left his wife and now he wanted to take the children away from her. Wangare was furious. He wouldn't even be able to feed Kiarie, or did he think that children don't need feeding? He could clear off and go back to where he came from.

He left before Kiarie returned home. Wangare finished the bottle on her own. When Kiarie returned, there was no food; his mother was drunk. She scolded him for not going to school and told him that he wouldn't get anywhere in life. He would become a good-for nothing like his father who had been there that afternoon.

"My father here? Where is he now? I want to see him," Kiarie had demanded.

"I told him to beat it; he's no good," Wangare said.

It was then that Kiarie had thrown the stone.

If you are building a house and a nail breaks,
do you stop building, or do you change the nail? —RWANDA PROVERB

HELPING OTHERS TO HELP THEMSELVES

Macharia is running off with a chicken leg, as his mother, Mary Njeri, shouts, "My son is a thief. He even steals a chicken from his own mother!"

Macharia, about ten years old, is a dirty, skinny boy with a cheeky face. At times this face can look very old, and at times it is full of joy and playfulness, as it is now.

He avoids me. He is a parkingboy and he finds it wiser not to talk to me, afraid that I will start talking about going to school. Macharia went to a school for about half a year. It was a good school, but he didn't feel he was really welcome; too often he was sent home. One day he was told that he was too dirty, the next time he was told that he must have a pair of shoes.

He wasn't a very good pupil but then, how can one learn on an empty stomach?

Now he spends most of his time on the streets of Nairobi. There are enough tourists who take pity on 'these poor little boys' and give them money, but without schooling they don't have much of a future. They don't stand any chance of getting a decent job. There is only a tough street life to teach them wisdom. They learn plenty all right, too many hard truths about society, but not nearly enough about joy and happiness in life.

Mary Njeri, Macharia's mother, sits in front of her shabby plastic hovel frying chicken innards and a few chicken legs on a charcoal stove. Her face is stern and tired although she isn't as old as she looks. I sit down with her.

She scolds Macharia. Mary has four children and her eldest, Macharia, is a parkingboy, a thief. She doesn't know the fathers of her children; they wouldn't care anyway. She has these children, but as far as Mary is concerned, I could have them if I liked, and certainly I could have Macharia. I can take him along right now, she assures me.

Mary is fed up with life, no husband, no job, four children and not a penny to her name. As she talks about it, she appears to grow more tired. She stirs the chicken, and her whole demeanour seems to sigh, "I don't know what to do any more; I am nobody and I am sick and tired of trying for more."

Two of her children, one six years old and the other eight, sit quietly. They watch and listen and they appear to be a little fearful.

A few members of the village committee join us and we talk together. Macharia on the streets is a bad thing indeed. We will try to help. We may be able to sponsor two children at school, if Mary herself will try to get the money for the school uniform of at least one child. After all, she does make some money now and again.

The two small children listen. For a moment their faces are full of hope, but then they realize that their mother is not interested any longer, and they walk away disappointed. Mary says that we can do whatever we like; she isn't going to do a thing any more.

Some other people join us and we all sit in a circle around the charcoal fire of Mary Njeri, some on old boxes and tins, others on their haunches. We talk together about helping. I try to explain our policy again, a policy which has been worked out with the village committee.

Poverty is crippling, and I compare it to a person having only one leg. Somebody with only one leg can give up on life, go and sit on the ground outside the post office and become a beggar—an unfortunate person to be pitied. We will certainly walk past him and not give him a single penny. Now, if a cripple will try to stand on his one leg, then we will do our utmost to support his effort and help him with a pair of crutches. But the cripple himself will have to learn to walk again. We cannot do the walking for him.

I think they understand what I mean. Certainly Mary Njeri knows that unless she makes an effort herself, the community is not going to help her.

Then an old drunk who is listening says, "I know someone with only one leg; can you get him a pair of crutches?"

Everyone laughs, except Mary. Sadly she looks at her dish on the fire, as if it isn't even worth the bother of eating. Again people talk and try to convince her that she can do something. Mary shakes her head. "The kids will become thieves in any case," she says.

Together with a few people we go to pay a call on Julia Wanjiru. She also has four children and she lives in a situation similar to Mary's, but she hasn't given up yet. Three of her children go to school. Somehow she got the money together for three school uniforms. It isn't my business to find out where she got the money. In this village of Kinyago, where she lives with more than a thousand of society's rejects, she has done a lot for her children.

Her little hut of plastic is kept clean. She is happy with her children even though now she tells them to clear off because she wants to talk to the visitors.

Then she tells us about her problems with getting a place in school for her fourth child. She doesn't have the money for a school uniform and neither does she have a birth certificate for the child; headmasters insist on that these days.

One of the men explains that a baptismal card will do instead. Yes, Julia has heard about that. "But, you see," and she looks accusingly at me, "I'm not married. I have no husband and you priests don't like to baptize our babies."

I feel ashamed that we have made regulations like this, and I am almost inclined to write a false baptismal card in order to help Julia. However, one of the men knows how to get hold of a birth certificate, but it will cost thirty-six shillings. This is a lot of money for Julia, so it is decided that it will be paid from our sponsorship fund, together with the money for the uniform. Everyone agrees that Julia has been trying to stand on the leg she has; she surely should be helped. Julia thanks us all, and I receive two eggs. I know that those skinny kids of hers would have been better off with them, but I don't feel I can tell her so. Why is it so easy to give, and yet so difficult to receive?

We continue to visit others; we talk with parents. We have had many meetings about our school sponsorship scheme. Members of the village committee explain the policy again and again.

I listen, and it all sounds so right—helping those who try to help themselves—not making people dependent, not just charity, not just giving a fish, but teaching people how to fish, in fact, making people aware of how to solve their own problems.

It sounds so good and it must be the only way. But, I wonder, is it really? I think of Mary Njeri and her disappointed children. Those children will go on the streets, just like their brother Macharia, that's for sure. Yet without Mary's co-operation we can't do much. We must stick to our rules, to our policy. And yet, the youngest child of Julia Wanjiru would get some attention and love, even if he didn't go to school. Mary Njeri's children have no future at all without a mother who has the strength to care, and certainly no chance at all if they can't go to school.

I feel very unsure about it all; helping people can be terribly complicated. After hours of talking and listening to people in such miserable conditions, I leave.

Macharia, the chicken-leg thief, leans against my car; he is entertaining some other children. He has eaten the chicken-leg down to the tendons. Now as he jerks them the foot seems alive and the toes pull together. Everyone thinks it is very funny, except his younger brother and sister. They look very unhappy. How can you laugh if you have just heard that next year too there will be no opportunity to go to school?

I decide that I will try and get the money for their school uniforms. I know that it isn't altogether wise, and that it is against our own principles, but then, wisdom and principles often make no sense in these idiotic situations in Kinyago.

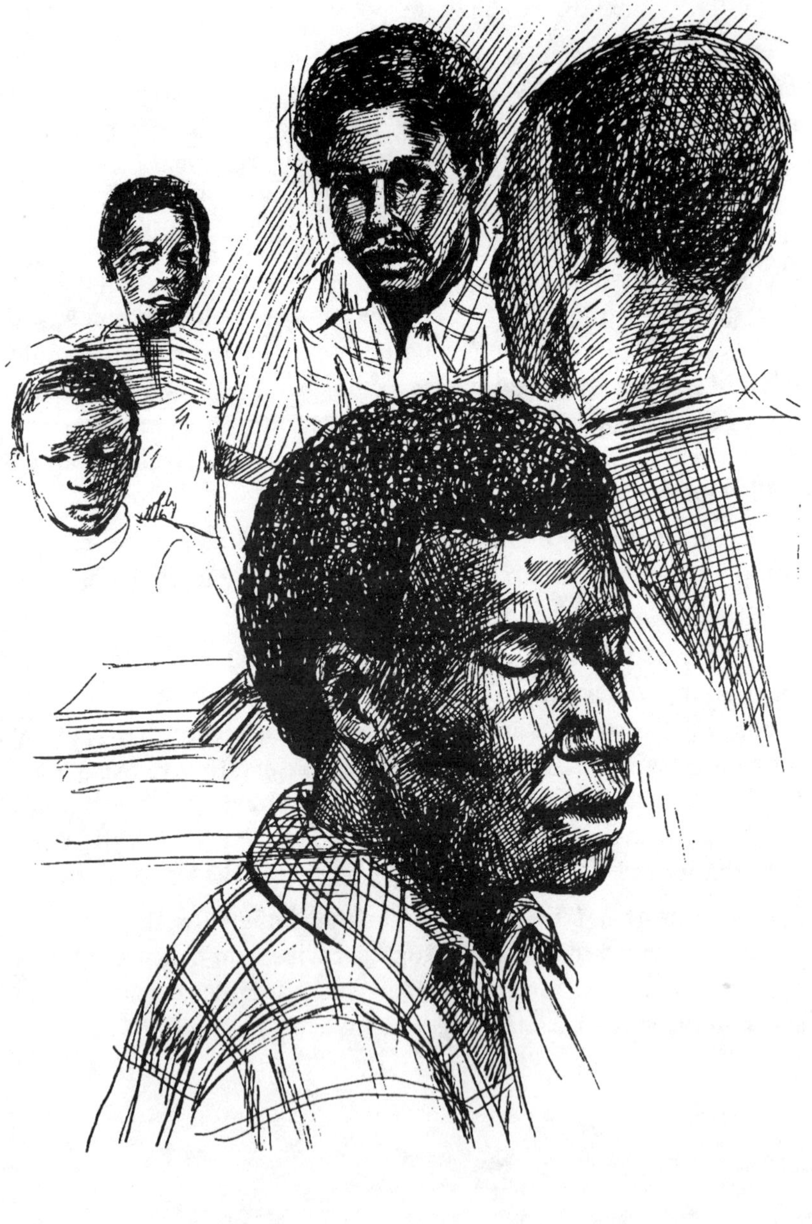

Nobody calls another's father 'Dad.' —KIKUYU PROVERB

YOUR OWN CHILD

"Do you know how many people can fit into a police cell?" asks John Mungai. I immediately think of the Guinness Book of Records—so many people squashed into a telephone box or a Volkswagen car. But John is not joking. He has just spent two days and nights in a police cell. No, John isn't a criminal, but you don't have to be a criminal to be picked up by the police in Mathare Valley. He had just been drinking a few bottles of beer to celebrate the birth of his son. He went outside to relieve himself and two policemen saw him. Urinating along a public road in Nairobi is an offence.

True, there are public toilets in Mathare Valley, but they are few and far between—John was just between. It was dark, and for John it was urgent. You certainly couldn't blame him for the lack of trees or bushes. John did what every other man in Mathare Valley would do, but he was caught by the police.

"What would you do if you lived here?" John asked one of the policemen.

It isn't wise to argue with the police; it is considered contempt of authority. The argument certainly was not appreciated and Mr. John Mungai was arrested. This wasn't the first time, for John isn't a meek person, and he absolutely refuses to hand out bribes to the police. He has too much self-respect and too little money.

"You weren't drunk, were you?" I ask.

"My son had just been born—and this one really is my own son. He even looks like me. Surely I'm allowed to celebrate that with a glass of beer?"

"Of course you are, John."

I happen to know how important this son is for teacher John Mungai. He has lived for many years in Mathare Valley, ever since he was a child. He had some schooling; he even went through secondary school, but getting educated was precarious: who could tell if there would be school fees next term? His mother would lose her job again or she would be caught hawking vegetables without a licence. There would be a choice—either pay the police and stay out of prison, or use the money for school fees for John. On those occasions when he was out of school John would try and study at home. He would sit in a corner with a book on his knees and his hands over his ears, trying to concentrate.

Then his mother would save some money or an uncle would help out and John would return to school. It was a long struggle. Now John is an 'unqualified teacher' in one of the Undugu Society's informal schools. He teaches boys and girls who would otherwise live on the streets. He teaches them not only how to read and write; but also how to survive in the slums. In this subject he is most certainly well-qualified.

The title 'unqualified teacher' bothers him. True, he has no certificate from one or other of the Teacher Training Colleges, but what is the qualification needed to understand and help these boys and girls?

John says, "If you haven't lived in the slums yourself, you will never understand them." He has lived there and still does today. And he has his doubts about those so-called experts. What on earth do they know about life in Mathare Valley? Do they know how it feels to be considered a thief or one of society's rejects? Yes, John has his doubts about the experts.

If you met John, you wouldn't think that he lives in the Valley. He has his own pride; he dresses well and a cigarette hangs loosely from his mouth. In fact he is a bit of a dandy. Clothes are important; clothes make a man. This is especially true if one doesn't have a big car or a beautiful house as status symbols.

John does have his own house though, on the borders of Mathare Valley. He saved money for it, designed it himself and built it with a few friends. It cost him a few hundred shillings. The walls and roof are made of cardboard nailed onto a frame of wooden poles. Nails alone would not hold the cardboard; it would tear when it started to rain, so under every nail he has put a reinforcing bottle-cap. A special feature in the construction is the double layers of cardboard with a small space in between them. Thus the house is cooler during the day and warmer during the night. For the outside walls John has used cardboard from boxes marked 'Fragile.' He has his own sense of humour. If you can no longer laugh at yourself, he finds, then everything is lost.

In this fragile house John lives a fragile marriage of sorts with his wife, Veronica. It is only in the last few weeks that he has felt that Veronica is truly his wife—she has given him a son. They have lived together for several years and this son is their second child. The first is not John's, he is sure of that, and Veronica has never claimed that it is.

Last year John and I talked about it for a whole evening. You might think that John was unhappy only because Veronica had been unfaithful to him. I thought along those lines, too. True, he did mind, but then he had been with other girls himself. John knows how life goes in Mathare Valley, and that wasn't what bothered him most.

It was a child in the house, the first-born, and this child not being your own, when you could have been the father. Yes, this was hard to bear for John. After all, one is a man in order to pass on life, or as John said that evening, "You are only a man if you pass on your own life, if you have your own child."

I, a celibate priest, felt that I wasn't much of a man in that case. "But you Europeans are different," John said. "You think you can bear fruit in different ways."

He didn't feel that he could marry Veronica before he had his own child by her. He loved her all right, but now he loves her even more, the mother of his son. Now he feels he is truly a man. One of these days he is going to talk to his future parents-in-law about marriage. They will respect him even more now that he has a son.

His friends respect him too; it is a pity the police did not. They locked him up and only once in twelve hours did he get an opportunity to go to the toilet. He was arrested for relieving himself along a public road; other men who were lying in the cell with him just urinated in the cell. It stank and was too crowded. The cell barely measured ten feet by ten feet, John assures me. He counted the men; apart from himself there were eighteen others.

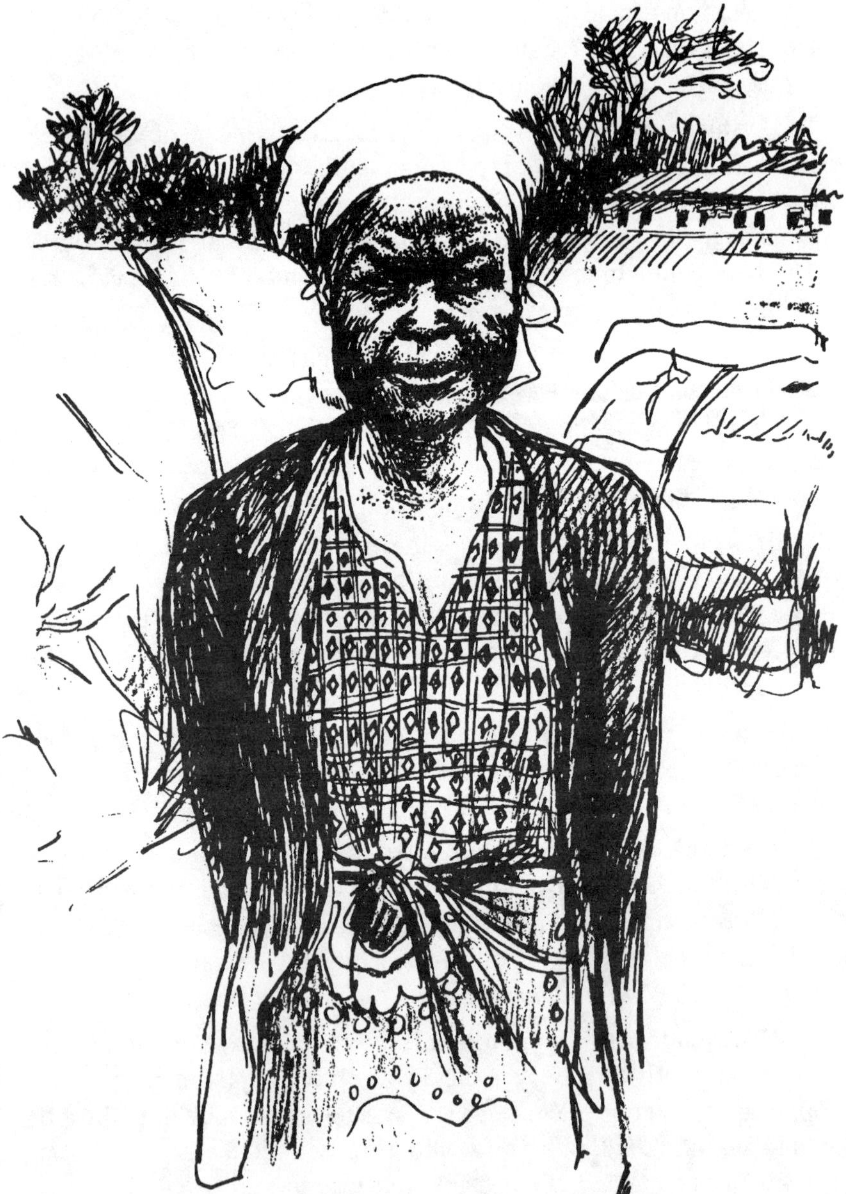

The woman who gets old without bearing a child will have nobody to draw water for her. —K̲ɪ̲ᴋ̲ᴜ̲ʏ̲ᴜ̲ ᴘʀᴏᴠᴇʀʙ

MUSINYA

Most people are Kikuyu in Kinyago Village, but in this poor quarter which I am visiting this morning, the inhabitants come from all over the country. A few come from Tanzania and Uganda. We talk in Swahili, a common language. There are cheerful greetings of *"Jambo"* and *"Habari,"* meaning "What's the news?" The news is always good and whilst I am assuring them that my news is also good, the old Musinya shuffles nearer, a broom under her arm. Musinya is certainly old, but I don't know her age in years. Her dress, which belonged to a Dutch housewife a few years ago, is worn out. Musinya has only the one dress. Her face is marked by a rough life, but it is a friendly face.

Musinya joins us. She puts down her broom; she takes her right arm in her left hand and we shake hands. She greets me in her own language and in its traditional manner. She knows that I understand it; for years I worked amongst her tribe. *"Mirembe, Mathayo"* — Peace be with you, Matthew, she says. *"Ulimulamu?"*—How are things in your life? or, Are you fully alive? she inquires.

I assure her that life isn't treating me too badly. It strikes me that this language sounds more civilized than Swahili. Perhaps Swahili is more a language for business since it came into existence during the slave trade. Its first greeting asks for news. Musinya doesn't do that. Her greeting, wishing me peace, reminds me of Christ's greeting, "Peace be with you."

It has become a small ritual that Musinya comes to greet me in her own language. People smile about it. In their eyes Musinya is a nice old lady. They don't begrudge her this small conversation in her own language; after all, she is the only one here of the Luya[14] tribe. Musinya doesn't have much, but it is more problematical that she does not have *anyone*. To be an old woman in Nairobi without children is hard. Only when Musinya is drunk, and that happens occasionally, does she talk about her daughter. Her daughter lives somewhere, almost four hundred miles away, in the neighbourhood of Busia. Perhaps she is married by now, which could mean that Musinya is a grandmother. Musinya doesn't really know, but the idea pleases her. There are many things Musinya doesn't remember too well; she cannot even remember how long she has been living here with these people. They have accepted her, in spite of the fact that she is of a different tribe. When I press her memory, Musinya replies, "Many years, almost since the death of my husband."

Yes, Musinya had a husband; he worked for the railways as a fireman, first of all in Kampala (Uganda) and later on in Nairobi. It was he who brought Musinya to Nairobi. Here she lived in a small house belonging to the railway company, a few miles from where she is presently living and trying to eke out an existence.

It wasn't a bad life; she had a husband with a job and she had a child. True, she was far away from her home, but every year the railway company gave her a free ticket to return home. When I ask her how long ago all this was, Musinya only says, "Many years, yes, many, many years."

Then one day Musinya's husband died. Musinya doesn't know who killed him. Musinya regards as nonsense the belief of the Europeans that you die of some disease or accident. People die because of one another or because of one of the forefathers. But then these forefathers also belong to us. Well, Musinya knows that she certainly didn't kill him. "He wasn't a bad man," she muses, and that usually means, "He was very good."

Musinya travelled with the body, together with her daughter, all the way to Busia in order to bury him there. People should be buried in their own homes. She was very lucky that the railway company paid for the journey.

But already during the funeral her troubles began. There, according to the customs of the Luya tribe, the wife does not inherit anything; indeed, she herself is inherited. Even a child does not belong to the mother but rather to the clan of the husband. This isn't altogether primitive nonsense. In the traditional pattern of life it provided widows with the best social security.

She was now inherited by one of her husband's brothers, who had two wives already. She went through the ritual, but she felt herself a city woman, independent, accustomed to the social structure of Nairobi rather than the ways of her kinsfolk in the countryside. This did not please the clan. She was even accused of being a witch and of having killed her husband.

Musinya didn't stay; she came back to Nairobi. Her people let her go, but her daughter had to remain behind, as the child of her brother-in-law. Back in Nairobi, Musinya found herself without a house. She had no income and she had to share a small room with a friend.

Several times she went to the railway company and asked for work. But they didn't need women, except to sleep with. When Musinya talks about men she always sounds a little bitter. In the end she went to the city market and got a job carrying vegetables. It was heavy work but it gave her a small income and she could contribute to the rent of the small room.

Then one day Musinya became ill, and that changed the 'friendship' with the woman with whom she was sharing the room. Unable to contribute anything towards the rent, she found herself out on the street. That was when Musinya arrived here and joined these other forgotten and rejected people.

When I first met Musinya here, a few years ago, she was very sick; almost dead. She could hardly stand and neighbours had to lift her from her bed of old rags when she had to go to the toilet.

"Chronically underfed," said a nurse who accompanied me one day.

"She doesn't eat any more; she only drinks a little chang'aa," neighbours said.

I gave the neighbours some money so that they could make sure that Musinya got something to eat. If I had given Musinya money at that time, she would only have bought chang'aa. Musinya also received a ration of milk powder, which was meant for children under five.

For a few months now this neighbourhood has had a small fund to help old people who are destitute. In Africa, you really are poor when you happen to be old and have no children. Children usually help their parents when they become old.

Our neighbourhood fund is largely in the hands of the village committee. They decide who is most in need. I can only hope that they are honest. In any case they are better judges in these matters than I. Musinya is on their list; she qualifies as 'old and destitute.' With twenty-two other people she receives twenty shillings each week. Of course this isn't much of a pension, but then people around her here survive on little more than this.

Musinya is quite prepared to do a little work for her money, so she sweeps the community hall. The community hall, a few poles and a roof, has no floor and what Musinya does, in fact, is raise a lot of dust. And so it is today when we enter, the place is full of dust. Musinya has just completed her task. We have come to discuss the Programme for the Aged with those most concerned, the old people themselves. Food has to be bought and prepared by neighbours for some of them, a little maize meal, cabbage, and instead of meat, *matumbo*—the intestines and stomach of the cow.

Others are able to manage the money themselves. Musinya is one of them. She comes forward and accepts the money with both hands. She thanks us in her own language. "*Murio*," she says, and everyone understands, "Thank you," and they smile about the old Musinya. However, the real meaning of "Murio" is "You are there." I hope that Musinya also means this.

Do not expect to draw blood from a fly. —Kikuyu proverb

KIRIMI

The water seller finds Kirimi quite impudent: she is not prepared to pay a shilling for twenty litres of water. Kirimi starts arguing that the people are being swindled by the water seller. They pay ten times more for water than I, who have running water at home. The boy wants to push his cart with eight drums of water farther up the road. Other women tell Kirimi that one shilling is the going rate these days for a drum of water. Kirimi pays grudgingly; she feels cheated. How could she know that the price of water had gone up again? She has been away, out of this misery, for seven months.

Kirimi is the mother of Hassan, Shahu and the twins. She is about thirty-five years old and has the looks of a gypsy woman. She has some Somali[15] blood in her, and her husband, with whom she came to Nairobi years ago, is a Somali. This same husband threw her on the street with her two children, Hassan and Shahu. It may be that she left him herself; I have heard only her side of the story.

For some time she roamed the streets with her two children, and she became a beggar. It was on the streets that she learned to be coarse and brazen, though by nature she is kind and gentle. There on the street she hit the bottle and there on the street she became pregnant again. She certainly didn't regard this as a blessing. Hassan and Shahu caused her trouble enough as it was. That was when she was stranded here in this village, with the other refuse of society. She gave birth to twins. Kirimi tried to care for them as well as she could, but it was hardly adequate. Again she went back onto the streets to beg and the children were badly neglected.

It was at this time that I came to know Kirimi, a ruined woman. But at the same time there was something of the warm-hearted gypsy in her. The neighbours often used to look after the children, but last year Shahu started to go on the streets, following the path of petty crime. Hassan became a scared little boy; he didn't know how to handle a drunken mother. Their hut was infested with jiggers. When Kirimi was home, she just sat outside her hut staring blankly into the distance. On other days she would wander half-drunkenly through the village, quarrelling with everybody, not taking any notice of her children. "Her head is not good any more," people would say.

It was at this time that we started to look for a home for Hassan. Kirimi didn't mind at all; she was sick. She had lots of stomach complaints; perhaps she had a bellyfull of all this misery. One can put up with it for a while, but not all the time. A week later she had a miscarriage. Kirimi ended up in a hospital run by Italian sisters. Physically, she recovered fairly quickly, but she remained very depressed, especially when people started talking about her going home. She was up and about whilst other patients had to stay in bed. Kirimi began helping them, running errands and bringing bedpans. It was a wise nun who encouraged her.

In the meantime the neighbours looked after Shahu and the twins. We discussed matters with the people who had taken Hassan into their home, and all three children were admitted, albeit reluctantly. Kirimi frequently asked after the twins.

Kirimi had been discharged from the hospital for quite some time now, but she didn't leave. She stayed and helped the sisters. Kirimi was good for the patients, for wherever she was, there was laughter, and laughter is a very good medicine. The sisters gave her a small room, plenty to eat and a little pocket-money. She helped with the laundry and ran errands for the patients.

Kirimi is a Muslim by birth, though she would go to the mosque only to beg. But at the hospital she became very pious, and her room was filled with pictures of Christ, Our Lady and the saints. Still an unabashed beggar, she begged the sisters for medals and rosaries. She didn't need all these herself, but she gave them to visitors whom she knew needed them very badly—people like me. She also managed to save something from her pocket-money which she gave for her children. Life was going well for Kirimi. Only once did things go wrong in all those months.

Five months ago she returned to Nairobi to visit her old friends in the slums. Kirimi arrived dressed like a lady—she had money nowadays. She was in high spirits, and didn't look at all as miserable as she used to. She had bought a bottle of chang'aa for the neighbour who looked after her children, and joined in drinking it. Why shouldn't she enjoy herself once in a while? They finished the bottle, and what happened after that Kirimi doesn't remember. She doesn't even remember where she stayed that night. Next day she arrived at the hospital dirty, ragged, sick and confused. For a few days she didn't work. Then we told her that she would get her children back if she wanted that, but that she must show that she could care for them properly. Kirimi wanted this very much indeed. She worked hard and became a ray of sunshine again for the patients.

A few months later Kirimi began to have stomach complaints again. The doctor who examined her asked whether or not she might be pregnant—she nearly beat him up. She *pregnant!* How could that be possible? Didn't she live like a nun? She didn't want to hear about it.

However, things slowly took a turn for the worse. It seemed that the patients were becoming very demanding. Kirimi became quarrelsome and she wanted to leave. Diana, who knows Kirimi very well, went with the village leader to visit her, and they talked with her for a long time. Kirimi decided to stay and resumed work.

Yesterday Kirimi returned to the slums; she still looks fairly clean. Her hut is still there and Kirimi is going to clean it with the water she finds far too expensive. She greets me somewhat sulkily. Yes, she has run away from that hospital, but it is not her fault; it is all the fault of that new sister. Kirimi had asked for medicine to treat her stomach-ache and vomiting, and then this sister too had said that she was pregnant. Kirimi is on the verge of tears as she tells me that this is impossible. She doesn't want to be offended any longer by those people in the hospital; that's why she has run away. If these sisters will not respect her, then she would rather be in the slums than in her nice little room at the hospital. I don't know what to say. Many people have tried to help this family, and we had the feeling that we were getting somewhere. None of us remembered that one night out, five months ago.

The doctor is certain; Kirimi is five-months pregnant.

The cattle shelter under the same tree with God.—AMBO PROVERB

IN THE MONASTERY

It is ten minutes to eight and Juja Road is still full of cars and people. Many cars don't bother to dim their headlights and the glaring light makes everything around us darker. People pass us like shadows. I press my bag, holding my Mass vestment and a bit of bread and wine, more firmly under my arm. I never feel very safe at night here on Juja Road. People get robbed all the time. It regularly happens that somebody is killed by a robber or by a car.

I feel a lot more at ease when I cross the open sewer and enter Mathare Valley. There are still crowds of people here, but they are at home, not rushing and not scared; I don't feel nervous here. I am among people. I am not alone in the crowd bordering Juja Road. Men stand talking together, women sit in front of their rooms, here people greet us. It is quite dark, save here and there the candescence of a lantern or a pressure lamp at a vegetable stall. The smells of cooked food, charcoal and urine hang in the air. Children join us and offer to carry my bag. By the time we arrive at 'Taizé' we are quite a group. It is here that we are going to celebrate Mass tonight.

Taizé is a small village in France, a monastery, a place of prayer, meditation, quietness and reflection. Here in Mathare Valley there is another 'monastery' of Taizé. The brothers have rented a scrapwood shack, and they live like their neighbours, separated by a thin wall of hardboard. Their roof leaks like the roof of the people next door. They pay too much rent just as everybody else around them.

Brother Denis, a monk in jeans, welcomes us at the door of the packed house. They have two rooms: a living-room which is also the reception-room and kitchen, and next to this, separated by a piece of canvas, there is a sleeping-room which is also a prayer-room and a chapel. Here Brother Denis, with the flexibility of a Frenchman and the endurance of a German, tries to be present for the people of Mathare Valley. A few Africans, brother candidates, have joined him.

It all started round about Christmas, 1978. Brother Roger Schutz, the founder of the Taizé community in France, came to Nairobi with about 25 young people from all over the world. To symbolize their solidarity with the poor, they lived for a few weeks among them in Mathare Valley. To some it seemed a naive gesture, but then it often takes a great deal of courage to be naive. Quite possibly, Christ would be called naive these days.

Denis and a few others remained. They stayed without much preparation, without big plans, without a job description. Denis is a qualified architect. Hardly anybody has a decent house in Mathare Valley. He has the courage not to start working, not to start projects, not to pour in money as we so often do. He and his fellow brothers have the time to be present with the people around them.

It is especially the children from the neighbourhood who come here, where they receive the time and attention which they don't get at home. Denis and the others organize games for them, perhaps a car rally with toy cars made by the children themselves, or they may take them for a walk to that other world outside the Valley. Through the children, they get to know their parents.

Now the dormitory-cum-prayer-room is packed with children and about 20 adults. In one corner of the room there is the Blessed Sacrament. A small African basket functions as the tabernacle. Above this is an icon from the Coptic Church, *Christ As A Brother to the People*. Brother Gregoire is also present. He sleeps here, but he works in town during the day. He earns a salary to support this community, working as a translator and French teacher. His work enables Denis and the others to be jobless and to do 'nothing.' The few belongings the brothers possess, their clothes, their blankets and their sleeping mats, hang on wires from the ceiling. In this way they are not eaten by rats. The roof is supported by two poles in the middle of the room.

I have to step carefully over several children in order to reach the small altar table. Many of the children demand attention; they try to shake hands with me as I attempt to put on my vestments. Martin van Asseldonk comes in. The children know him, and several want to sit on his lap, but he only has place for two. The wooden shutters are open, uniting us with the people and the noise in the street. A young man, a bit drunk, leans through one of the windows, debating whether or not he will attend the service.

With an opening song we easily drown the noise of the radio next door. This radio is always on when we celebrate Mass here. This evening we celebrate the feast of the previous day, the feast of Peter and Paul, two pillars of the early Church.

I try to find out who is called Peter, Paul, Paulina, Petronella, Petra or Paula. This is their feast day, too. Hands go up and we applaud all of them. The face of a small Paul or Peter in front of me lights up in response. They start singing again. No, they don't sing solemnly or beautifully as one might expect in a monastery of Taizé. These children and adults sing the way life is in Mathare Valley: raw and loud. The children are not nice, sweet little ones. They are restless, in some ways demanding, craving the care and attention to which they have a right, but which they do not get in their broken homes. At times when I get here, I wish we could do something very beautiful, so that they all would look and listen in amazement. But they aren't easily impressed. A boy of fifteen beats the drums vigorously, as if he is accompanying a troupe of traditional dancers.

We read about those two disciples of Christ, Peter and Paul, whose lives are to be an inspiration to us today. At the same time, people can listen to the news on the radio next door. They have a choice. The kids seem to be interested in those two disciples.

The two poles in the middle of the room have been dressed up today. By means of blankets, faces drawn on old paper, cement sacks, and beards made of sisal, they have become contemporary statues of Peter and Paul. Brother Denis explains. They are two pillars, not of concrete but of flesh and blood. They supported the early Church. It was not a church of concrete but a Church of flesh and blood, a Church of people. Each had his temperament, each had his own character, vision and commitment to build communities. Both had to pay for this with their lives. Denis tries to explain this and what it might mean to us. At the same time somebody else is trying to sell us Blue Band margarine on the radio. I must admit, technically, the man who is advertising Blue Band is much better than Denis. But we easily shut him up with a very loud version of the Creed. The advertiser can't beat that one. These people certainly believe in a lot more than just bread and butter, or Blue Band margarine.

Passers-by stop and look through the window. The half-drunk man, who seems to have decided to stay, scratches his head thoughtfully as we pray for people who are in distress. Now and again he joins in with the singing. Many others have gathered at the window and the service is now half in the street.

The wishing of peace to one another before Holy Communion is chaotic; everybody wants to shake hands with everybody else, and all, especially the children, climb and fall over one another in an effort to do this. Together with brother Denis, I distribute communion; for some communicants we have to reach very far over all these singing children. People hand the chalice to one another.

During the last song, after the blessing, some adults and Brother Gregoire start leading the children out. Some don't want to leave; they protest that the song isn't finished yet. The drummer has a last go at that drum of his and the grown-ups start looking for their shoes and slippers. They talk together. They know each other, meeting here as they do, every Wednesday. I haven't said much to them tonight; the service was directed more towards the children. But the adults can probably still understand that language; after all, they were children once. I hope they haven't forgotten that.

A baby goat in the street nervously bleats for its mother. These children don't seem in a hurry to go back and look for their mothers. One of them is walking around with a piece of St. Peter's beard. I shake hands with lots of people. A child wanting some attention asks, "Father Mathew, what is your name?"

As I walk home I still think about the service in the monastery of Taizé. Beautiful, devout, solemn, meditative—none of these words has anything to do with it. Perhaps the words *real* or *true to life,* describe it better. Whatever the case, this liturgy doesn't stand apart from everyday life in Mathare Valley. In many ways it reflects it.

I also think to myself that somebody out there has lost some fleas; they seem to have found a home with me. I am itching like mad!

It is not the mother's will to have bad offspring. —KIKUYU PROVERB

NIMESHINDWA

"Electina herself has beaten that child. I would run away as well!" Musyoki shouts out.

"Don't be ridiculous. Muthoni doesn't respect her mother. She even threw stones at her mother. What kind of child is that?" Wamboyi defends Electina.

"Come on, Muthoni isn't a bad child; she is only twelve years old."

"That child, you can call her good? You should have your head examined. She even stays out at night."

"Her mother is a whore. How else did she get five children without a husband?" The last remark is again Musyoki's; she is in a quarrelsome mood and it seems she is determined to have a good row.

Electina, Muthoni's mother, sits amongst the rubbish next to her hut of polythene and cardboard. She is still rather young and at times she even looks pretty, but now she looks tired and old. She continues to sew a doll while her neighbours quarrel about her and make judgements about her and her daughter, Muthoni. For a few months now she has been working with a women's group, making cloth dolls. No, not for her children, but in order to sell them. Her own children only have sticks and old tins for toys. She goes on sewing, apparently calm, but her face is tense and weary-looking. With that last remark of Musyoki, that she is a whore, her mouth twists as if she has been slapped in the face.

"Electina, where is your daughter now?" I ask. She shrugs her shoulders; she doesn't know.

"She was staying with her aunt at Kariobangi, but she has even run away from there. Doesn't that show what kind of a girl she is?" one of the neighbours cuts in.

"It's all Electina's fault; she took Muthoni to the police," Musyoki answers.

This Musyoki seems to be determined to have a good row. I feel like telling her a few things, but I suggest to Electina that we talk further in her hut. To talk here, with these jabbering women around, doesn't make much sense. In her poor hovel Electina offers me an empty car-battery to sit on. The teacher, Simon, who came along with me, sits on an empty tin. Electina sits on the bed, still sewing the doll. It is a pitiful sight; her youngest child, who is about one, is crying, the three-year-old twins are tugging at her dress. Electina doesn't pay attention to them. She looks so terribly tired. Now, however, she talks.

"My girl Muthoni reproaches me because we are poor, she reproaches me because I haven't got a job. How could I go to work? Even if I could get a job, I, with five children... Muthoni only remembers the evenings when I couldn't give her anything to eat. She forgets that most evenings we go to bed with full stomachs. True, we are poor, but Muthoni doesn't give me a hand with the other four children. Muthoni is my eldest child, my first-born. I have tried everything, *lakini nimeshindwa*—but I am defeated." Tears are in her eyes.

These are just a few of the sentences which have remained with me after the talk with Electina this morning. She admits that in despair she has beaten Muthoni. It is also true that she went to the police, the time that Muthoni ran away and slept in the street. She had expected that her eldest child would help her; perhaps she expected it too soon. Muthoni surely could see that she couldn't manage everything on her own. And then these twins... People say that twins don't bring luck. Europeans are inclined to call that superstition. Electina knows that this has nothing to do with superstition. She never considered letting one of the twins die, as is often customary. But to breast-feed two babies when you don't have enough milk for one, when the mother herself isn't fed properly, that isn't an easy matter. Electina herself has been very sick, and it was a long time before her twins began to look anything like normal, healthy children. And Muthoni, she didn't want to help, she only wanted to go to school like other children. In the end she gave in and let Muthoni go to one of the informal schools run by Undugu.

"But has that improved things?" she asks, looking reproachfully at the teacher. We are now searching for Muthoni who has run away.

"Do you want us to bring Muthoni here if we find her?" we ask.

Electina ponders and in the end she shakes her head. "*Nimeshindwa*—I am defeated," she says.

When we get up to leave and search for Muthoni, Electina adds, "Don't believe Musyoki. It is true, I have no husband, but I am not a whore."

I believe Electina. She is not a whore. She is poor. She has five children. So often we think that people are poor because they have too many children. I become more and more convinced that Electina and others have so many children because they are poor. Children are a kind of social security, an investment for the future. Is this why Electina is so disappointed that her firstborn, Muthoni, doesn't live up to her expectations?

An unmarried woman also feels that she should have children, although Electina never wanted to have twins. Quite possibly, men have used Electina as a whore, but I believe Electina when she says she is not one.

Together with Simon, the teacher, I go and look for Muthoni. Muthoni is a lanky girl of twelve. She has been in school for nearly a year now. She tried hard, she was a good pupil, but she could be a very quiet girl. She had stayed away a few times before, but in the last four days, she has not shown up at all.

We drive to Kariobangi to see her aunt who might know more. The aunt is not at home and Muthoni is not there either. We ask around. Muthoni was seen yesterday at a tea kiosk, and it is thought she slept there. We go and talk with the kiosk-owner, a kind, elderly

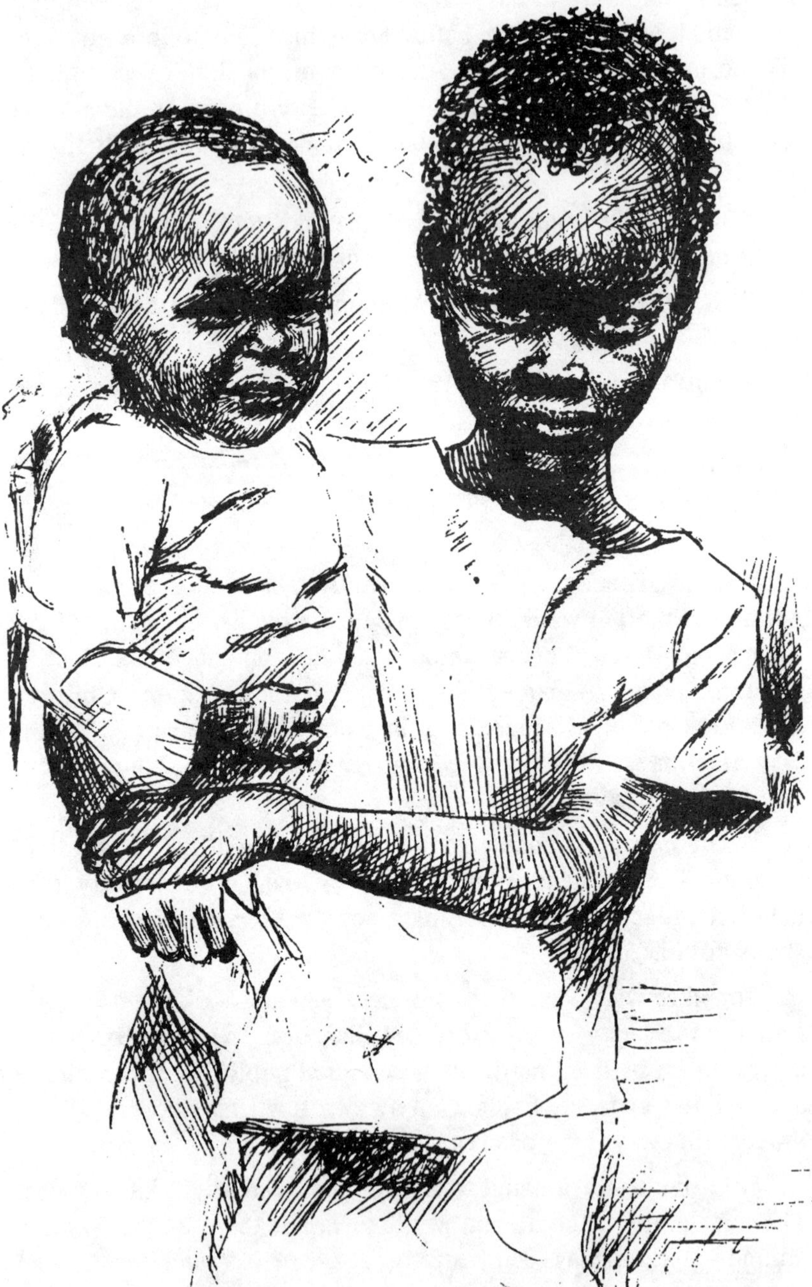

man, it turns out, who had looked after Muthoni for a few days. During the night he had heard somebody crying in the field behind his kiosk. He went to look and found Muthoni, a frightened little girl; she had been afraid, alone in the dark. He had given her some tea and let her sleep on the floor of his kitchen.

"She is a smart girl," he says, "but she didn't want to tell me where her home was. No, she didn't want to go home."

This morning he had found out where she belonged. He had given her some money for bus fare. Muthoni only cried. She didn't want to go back to her mother. She had said her mother didn't want her; her mother only wanted an *aya* (a girl who looks after children). Where did she want to go then? She had mentioned a girlfriend in Pumwani. In the end she had walked off, a small girl all alone in the endless slums of Nairobi. Simon thinks that he might know her girlfriend in Pumwani. We drive to Pumwani and we ask around. We find the girlfriend, but she hasn't seem Muthoni.

It is now evening and it is cold. Little Muthoni roams the town somewhere, like a scared stray kitten. She is not the only one wandering around Nairobi. It is not likely that she will meet another kind kiosk owner. Child prostitution is common. She certainly hasn't gone back to her mother.

Muthoni is scared and alone in the night. The nights in the streets of Nairobi are not friendly, especially for small girls.

Nimeshindwa—I am defeated. That is what Electina said too.

There is no phrase without a double meaning. —Kenyan proverb

MATATU

Once again I am stuck in a traffic jam. They are a common feature in Nairobi these days. I am not the most patient person, and to get over my frustration I take up the sport of 'matatu watching.' Now, I am not a great fan of the matatu. The few times I travelled in them I found it a harassing experience. True, I got to town, but I was squashed, and felt afraid of the speed at which the driver overtook other cars. I didn't share the driver's confidence in his brakes. It is not the driver's skill that I admire, but rather the names they have given to their vehicles.

After watching them for a few weeks, I have begun to discover several classes of matatu drivers. As I am waiting for the traffic to move again, one cheeky driver passes me on the left, which means he is driving on the pavement, (sidewalk). On the matatu's side is written, *Mind Your Own.* For me that one belongs to the second class, the disillusioned ones. The first class are the young and fast drivers; they still have a dream and are a little foolish; they are even prepared to fool themselves. Their old Volkswagen Combi or the third-hand Nissan bus are not really what they appear to be. In their eyes these are what they have baptized as 'taxis.' I see names like, *Oriental Express, Moonwrecker Escort,* or *Sex Queen*—all suggesting speed and excitement.

Next to me I see an overloaded taxi. The young driver, with a big cowboy hat, is sitting behind his steering wheel like a confident pilot. His matatu is called *Jumbo Jet.* He would love to jet away, but he is stuck here just as I am. He keeps his engine revved up, ready to take off as soon as there is room to squeeze through. Others in this class become globetrotters as they drive from Kariobangi to town. They sport beautiful names like *Akapulco Tours; Mecca Tours;*

Africa Safaris or *Rainbow Tours*. It all sounds beautifully exotic of course, but they will still break down. The passengers have to push and they scold the driver or demand their money back. Some drivers stick to their dreams: they let the people shout and they continue to fly their jets.

Others have had enough of it all and have started to realize that they are driving just an old ramshackle Bedford through a crowded city. These are in the second class. They tell their passengers and the Nairobi world a thing or two, especially that they don't want any more quarrelling and shouting. They name their matatus *Mind Your Own, Leave the Gossip, Sitaki Maneno*—I don't want an argument. Where there are matatus there is a lot of shouting, a lot of gossip among the passengers, and arguments about who picked whose pocket. One driver, really fed up with all this, has written on the side of his matatu, *Heri uchawi kuliko fitiua,* which could be translated, 'We would rather have witchcraft than an argument.' Another one in this class, pleading for a bit of kindness, has called his taxi, *No Love, No Money*. But one of his colleagues who has experienced the hard Nairobi life, probably with his wife living back home in the rural area, has changed these words slightly. On his taxi I read recently, *No Money, No Love*.

These impulsive young men mature too. Running a matatu is not easy. The turnboys have to hang onto the back door, shouting out which route they are taking, they pack the passengers in and collect the money. Moreover, matatus break down. Maybe some of them wouldn't mind another job, but they know only too well how scarce jobs are in Nairobi. They realize that this is at least work. Such sentiments come out in the names of their vehicles.

Common names are *Kazi ni Kazi*—Work is Work, and *No Work is Misery*. Others seem to encourage themselves or the public with *Usiongope Kazi*—Don't Be Afraid of Work. I don't think these matatu drivers become rich; one really old matatu which is seen often in Eastleigh is called *Kwaheri Utajire*—Goodbye Wealth. Another one is called quite bluntly, *Survival*.

The traffic jam dissolves and I try to rush home, but I am overtaken by an old Bedford van which stops as soon as it has passed me and lets out a few passengers. It has no brake lights, and I am pretty sure that it would not stand up to a police-check. The driver seems to know that, too, because above the back door, I read: *In God We Trust.* Here is a class on its own: the theologians. Yes, they drive matatus too. Their belief is no longer grounded in mankind, nor in technology. Their matatus are repaired in open-air garages and you really can't rely on their mechanics. So these matatu drivers have turned to God as their last hope. In this class you find names such as, *May God Save Us,* and, *Have Faith in God!* I am uncertain whether that is the prayer of the driver or of the passengers! These people don't write books about theology; they state their religious convictions quite simply on the front and on the back of their taxis. Here are a few more names which fall into this category: *God is Good; Mungu ni Moja*—God is one; *God Saves.* Another famous one, with a somewhat reckless driver, shows clearly the missionary influence in Kenya; the taxi is called *Christ Is the Answer.* I wonder whether anyone has ever thought of what the question might be?

I don't know who the real owners of all these matatus are—certainly most of them don't belong to the drivers. But there is one category which I like to think belongs to the family—perhaps a small family business. Dad himself may be behind the steering wheel. Their names refer to the family. This probably works two ways; it reminds both the driver and the passengers of home. One sees names like *Family Success; No Home Without Mama,* or *Mtoto wa Mama*—Mother's child. When that engine starts spluttering again both the driver and his passengers will repeat the name of another matatu, *Take Me Home.* In this class I also put *Sauti ya Baba*—Father's voice. Frequently, because the operator has had to borrow from an uncle to buy the matatu, as a token of thanks he may call it *Uncle Joe Express.*

Maybe some of my interpretations are out in left field, but then I only recently started matatu watching. It helps me to get over the frustration of being stuck yet again in Nairobi traffic. There is still a lot to learn. One colourfully-painted old Datsun pick-up appeals to me in particular; it has painted on it, *I Am Still Searching...*

Sorrow is like a precious treasure, shown only to friends.
—MADAGASCAR PROVERB

DEAD AND BURIED

Njoki was one of the many small children who always come to shake hands with me when I arrive in Kinyago. Until a few days ago Njoki was just one of the many children who together run around in Kinyago, like a herd of little goats. Together they may try to catch a chicken or congregate about me when I am trying to talk with someone. Giggling, they touch my arm—we have hair on our arms; Africans don't have any. They also try to 'clean' my car with their grubby hands. After they have finished, the car really does look dirty!

Njoki was one of them. About three years old, she ran along with the others, baring her little bottom to the world.

Last week Njoki was sick. She had fever and diarrhea. Clad in only a few rags, she was lying rather forlornly in the big bed of her mother, Wamboyi. I told Wamboyi to give Njoki a lot to drink, water with a bit of salt and sugar. Wamboyi would have preferred Njoki to have had an injection. People expect miracles from injections.

The next day I found Njoki worsening, but Wamboyi simply didn't have the time to take her to hospital. Wamboyi never has much time to look after children; her small vegetable trade takes nearly all her time. Having no husband, she has to face things alone. Njoki is what people often call 'a child of ten shillings.'[†]

When Njoki was nearly dead, the neighbours intervened and told Wamboyi to go to hospital with the child. That was where Njoki died. She is now in the mortuary in town.

[†] Cf. p. 64

I now know Njoki and everyone in the village of Kinyago knows her too. She could not be buried straight away because Wamboyi did not have the money to pay for the funeral. A permit is needed from the District Commissioner to collect money. Some neighbours purchased one and yesterday they were busy collecting money.

Njoroge sat behind the table with an exercise book. Everybody contributed a few shillings; the name and the amount were written down. I made a small contribution and I agreed to lead the service. A few hundred shillings was collected, but that was only enough for the coffin. The neighbours decided that it should be a coffin with a small window in the lid. People should be able to see Njoki's face before she is buried. Njoki never had her own bed, but now that she is dead she will at least have a good coffin. The funeral is postponed for a day because they don't have enough money for the transportation. Njoroge now leaves the village with his exercise book and the permit of the D.C. and he sits by a busy road to ask passers-by for a small contribution. Not many refuse. They know that a funeral in town is very expensive.

I visit Wamboyi to offer my sympathy. She is sitting in front of her hut peeling bananas; now that her child is dead she doesn't go to her work. Njoki was her youngest; she still has two other children, though another child died a few years ago. Her face is stern, but her eyes are filled with sadness. She is in her early thirties.

Not knowing what to say, I bungle about with words. Words soon sound very hollow at such occasions. "God gives life. He can also take it back. Who am I, a human being, to oppose God?" says Wamboyi.

Today is the day of the funeral. I go to meet some of the village leaders at the mortuary. Some money has to be paid before the body is released. They pay, and the expensive coffin is brought in with a window in the lid. Then, however, the matatu driver demands an extra hundred and fifty shillings for the trip to the graveyard. He knows that the people have no choice. This makes me very angry and I offer to drive the body to the graveyard myself. It isn't a real solution, of course. I can take only a few people in my small car, but my offer is a great help in the ensuing bargaining. The driver realizes that he isn't quite God Almighty and is satisfied with an extra fifty shillings.

When I arrive at the graveyard in Langata, forty to fifty people from Kinyago are already there. They have come by bus. Wamboyi stands among them, straight-faced, almost grim. Three young prostitutes stand at the head of the group, all dressed in black, high heels, and black veils on their heads. They lend a certain dignity to the group.

Five graves for children are already prepared and money has to be paid again before we get one. Njoroge counts out the shillings. The small coffin is put on the freshly dug red soil. The window is opened and everybody has a last look at Njoki.

It is all too much for Wamboyi and she nearly starts to cry. Two women lead her away. Kikuyu women are not supposed to shed any tears at a funeral. They may do that later, when they are among women only. There are tribes with different customs: where everyone cries and weeps at a funeral.

I don't quite know what to do; must I start the funeral without Wamboyi? Nobody else seems to know which ritual has to be followed at a graveyard in the city. The ritual of the country, which they are used to, doesn't fit in here any more.

Fortunately, Wamboyi returns and one of the leaders makes a long speech in Kikuyu, which I don't understand, but the others look impressed. At the end of the speech he looks at me, telling me that it is now my turn.

I propose to start with a reading from the Bible; most of us are Christians of one or other persuasion. One of the three ladies in black comes forward and offers to read. After this we pray together and I bless the coffin and the grave. The song we try to sing is blown about this large graveyard by the wind. Wamboyi stands there stony-faced.

As we begin to lower the coffin into the grave, people come and tell us to hurry up; another funeral procession is waiting. With big spades the grave is filled with red soil. A cross, two wooden slats, is brought forward. 'Njoki, child of Wamboyi,' is inscribed upon it. One of the well-dressed young ladies in black lays a wreath of expensive flowers on the grave.

Now we leave.

Njoroge is counting out his shillings again; people receive their bus fares home. I hear later that Njoroge spent nearly a thousand shillings on this funeral. Not even half that amount was spent on Njoki in her whole lifetime. In the slums, death is considerably more expensive than life.

Living is worthless for one without a home. —ETHIOPIAN PROVERB

A COAT FULL OF LICE

Lekonzo is demolishing old Hassan's hut. Lekonzo trades in second-hand and third-hand plastics. Hassan won't need this place any more. It isn't really a hut, more a kind of a den made of all sorts of bits and pieces. It would become only a hiding-place for snakes now that Hassan has gone away.

The pieces of plastic which are still of some use are folded and put aside. The rest Lekonzo throws on a heap of rubbish. There I also see the old army overcoat which Hassan wore for years. The last few years it served as an extra blanket.

'The coat of an old man is filled with lice,' is a Swahili saying. This old coat has seen a lot in life; Hassan's was not a smooth one. He left the coat behind yesterday when he quit the city and returned to the countryside of his birth, a little place near Kitale which is about three hundred miles from Nairobi. He was born by the roadside or perhaps along the path to the river. His first name is Wingira, which means 'Born on the wayside.'

His father was a tenant on the farm of a white settler. He was paid little, though he received a ration of maize meal and he was allowed to cultivate a small piece of land for himself and his family. The hut which Wingira grew up in was not his father's but belonged to the white settler, as did the school he attended for a few years. Besides learning to read and write, he received his first religious classes in this school, and he was baptized Benson by the parson who regularly visited the farm.

As a child he worked in the farm smithy. At first he only looked after the fire, but later on he turned his hand to the forge. Just like

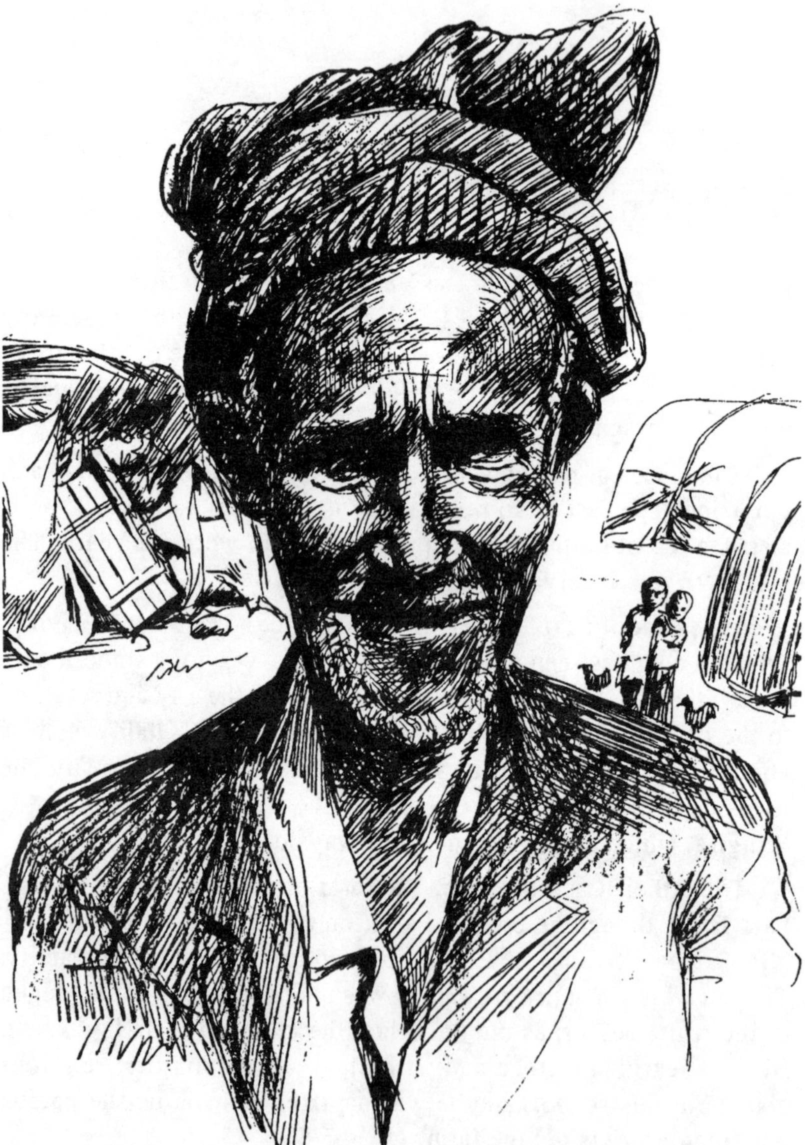

his father he worked for a low wage, a ration of maize meal and a small piece of land for himself, Anna and their three children.

Benson knew just as well as his wife that this was at best an indifferent life. He wasn't much of a fighter, but that Anna should call him a slave was very hard to swallow. It wasn't an easy marriage; Anna did not respect him. How could she? He was a man without his own house, without his own homestead, without his own cows, and that is not much of a man in the lands of the Bantu people. But what could he do about it? He did not like rows with Anna and he didn't want them with the farmer. It was true that others went to fight for land, for freedom, but Benson wanted only peace and no fighting.

Anna remained discontented. Other men would have beaten their wives in such a situation, but Benson didn't beat Anna.

Then one day he left his family and went to Nairobi. He had heard that the wages in the city were very much higher than those on the farm. He wanted to earn the money for a piece of land, school fees for his children, a house for himself and Anna, and perhaps even enough money for a second wife. Quite possibly it was to escape Anna's nagging tongue too!

In Nairobi he ended up in the African quarter, Pumwani. In those days Nairobi was divided into areas for Whites, Asians and Africans or "natives" as they were then called. Pumwani means 'Breathe freely' or 'Take it easy.' That is what the place truly meant for many Africans who worked for the Whites or the Asians, under whom they all too often could not breathe freely.

Benson moved in with friends of some acquaintances who also came from Kitale. He lived in one of the narrow streets that have a gutter in the middle, above which children neatly relieve themselves. The artisans sit and work in the open shops, and at night meat is roasted at street corners. Old men sit together and talk or play draughts whilst looking after small children whose mothers are working. The first major group to inhabit this area was of people from the coast who built the railway. The prostitutes followed, but they were nicely confined to the back streets. They were and are visited by the many unmarried men, or by men like Benson who had left their wives in the country.

Benson tried to find a job but met with little success. One needs influential friends to get a job, but he had only uninfluential friends. In the end he started his own small business; after all, he knew something of blacksmithing. He would sit in the street and repair pots and pans with a few simple tools. He borrowed some money, bought a few old barrels and started making charcoal stoves. Living among the Muslims, he borrowed money from them, and they were his clients. He adjusted to their way of life. Everybody would go to the mosque in the evening, so Benson bought himself a white cap and called himself Hassan. He was a Muslim, though not a fanatic. He certainly couldn't afford four wives—he remained far too poor for that.

Hassan worked hard, but he wasn't a good businessman. In order to be a good businessman, one must be able to compete, to fight. Hassan couldn't fight. He simply made a living and was able to pay the rent for his small room, as the landlords in Pumwani were not yet so wretched as to overcharge.

His piece of land, his house and going back to Anna and the children as a successful man remained a very distant dream. Only at the end of the sixties did things begin to improve. Business went well and Hassan had started to save his first few shillings.

Then people from the Town Planning Office arrived. Pumwani was judged to be uninhabitable. The slums were going to be demolished and flats would be built. A large section of Pumwani was demolished, the part where Hassan lived. The flats which were erected were indeed beautiful, but what Hassan earned in two months as a blacksmith would not pay the rent for one month. With many others, he found himself homeless. His business began to collapse and his eyesight was deteriorating. He had a cataract in one eye and was partially blind in the other.

Others, homeless like Hassan, built their own illegal houses of plastic and scrapwood a few hundred yards farther on. In the beginning Hassan joined them, but when the bulldozers came and everything was demolished again, Hassan felt defeated. Others fought on and rebuilt their houses, but not Hassan; he wasn't a fighter. He needed a place to sleep so he stuck a few bamboo sticks into the ground and then threw a few pieces of plastic over them. It was nothing like a hut or a home, but it protected him against the rain.

Thirty years in Nairobi had left him old and overwhelmed. Now and again he received a meal at the mosque in Pumwani. He had forgotten his old dream. Jan Reusen, a colleague of mine, included Hassan in a programme for destitute, old people. Last month we gave him a small sum of money so that he could improve his shelter and make something decent of it. He bought a few poles but he certainly did not start building with much enthusiasm. The next day he was drunk, probably on the money we had given him.

Hassan left yesterday; he returned to the land, to Anna and the children. He couldn't have managed on his own, to go back to his home from the city as a failure; that would have been almost impossible. One of his sons came to look for him. Anna was sick and they expected her to die very soon. But Hassan and Anna had not made their peace, and that would have been a terrible state in which to die, for then even after death there would be no peace. Hassan went along with his son; he didn't want a row, and he wanted to make peace with Anna.

He left behind his old army coat. Yes, the coat of an old man is full of lice.

He who asks questions cannot avoid the answers. —Cameroon proverb

CRIME

There was a lot of shooting in our neighbourhood during the night. At first it sounded far away, then there were a few shots nearby. All of a sudden the shots of a machine gun rattled out very close to us. I got up and noticed that one of my colleagues, Augustine, had got out of his bed as well. It now sounds as if a small war is going on around us. Augustine is more acquainted with the sound of guns, because he was in Uganda for many years during the war there. But that doesn't make him any less nervous than I am. He decides to phone the police.

"There is some shooting going on in Eastleigh," he tells the police.

"Nothing to worry about. It's us," the police reply.

At breakfast the cook tells us that three people have been shot. They were thieves, he has heard, and he goes off to the kitchen to wash the dishes. He is not particularly impressed: thieves should be shot, is how he sees it.

Abungu has heard the shooting too. For him it is not as simple as for our old cook. Abungu is a teacher in one of our informal schools. He finds it criminal that suspected thieves are shot by the police. He finds it a criminal world in which he lives anyway—especially on mornings like this one.

Abungu is mixture of philosopher and a freedom fighter. He has his own way of looking at things and he is not reluctant to speak his mind. As I walk into the school office he greets me with a broad smile. He opens with, "Good morning, criminal."

"What have I done wrong today?"

"We are all criminals," Abungu says, "every one of us. I sell chang'aa for my mother. It is forbidden by law, so I am a criminal. But so are you, don't fool yourself. You, as a Mzungu, you use a far greater portion of the world's energy than you have a right to. I happen to think that is criminal, too."

Abungu says it all with a big grin on his face, but he knows *he* runs the risk of being arrested, whilst I am in no such danger. He pulls the green army beret, his freedom-fighting self, over one ear and he starts philosophizing.

"Has it been proved that the three who were shot are guilty?'

There is a fire in his eyes now, and I feel like saying that I didn't shoot them, but Abungu goes on. "Stealing is against the law, but whether or not you are shot for it depends on who does the stealing and from whom, and what is stolen," Abungu says.

He gives me a lecture. Crime for him is more than an act against the law. That may be the definition one finds in a dictionary, but for Abungu that is not good enough. He has been studying this matter for a whole day with some other teachers.

He searches through a heap of papers on his desk. Yes, here he has got it—a list of 'crimes' that his pupils are acquainted with. Stealing, robbery, bribery, child abuse, drug addiction, abortion, unlicensed business, prostitution, robbery with violence, pickpocketing, smuggling, trespassing, etc. It is a very long list and it classifies nearly all the people in Mathare Valley as criminals. Abungu himself comes from a family of criminals. His mother brews chang'aa. Just imagine that—his mother a criminal. She brewed chang'aa to give him, Abungu, a decent education. He got a good education; he went to school, but he still lives in this 'criminal' world. All this is against the law, but is it criminal? Abungu would rather call it by another name—poverty.

Real crime, that is a different matter for him. "Is it not a crime that people have insufficient to eat? That they have to live here in these dreadful conditions, that ordinary human rights are being denied? That these three have been shot without a trial—is that not a crime?"

Abungu fires off these questions; he doesn't expect an answer from me. For him the answer is already clear.

I know Abungu as a very understanding man, who cares for his pupils and is always willing to help. But he doesn't want to be just a Good Samaritan. He also wants to see where these robbers have gone to.

He rummages through the papers on his desk again. Then he reads: "Del Monte—also called Kenya Canners. Labour force is 10,000, of which 7,000 are casual workers. They earn 450 Kenya shillings per month, of which K.Shs.200 is deducted for housing. Often four workers live in one room. The chairman of Del Monte earns 3.5 million. Del Monte controls over 80,000 acres of fertile Kenyan land of which less than one-third is planted. Is it correct that vast tracts of Kenyan land are turned over to multi-nationals for export crops while some people here face starvation? Until recently Del Monte paid no Kenyan tax."

Abungu nonchalantly throws the paper back onto his desk.

"None of it is against the law," says Abungu, "but is this not criminal?"

Many of the children being taught by Abungu have come into contact with the police. They have committed one or other of those little 'crimes.' But Abungu knows that the big criminals in Kenya don't live in Mathare Valley or in any of the other slums.

A few days ago we had a tremendous rainstorm in Mathare Valley. Mathare River flooded, houses were washed away, and people were made homeless. "Do you remember?" Abungu asks.

Of course I do. My own colleagues couldn't come home by car because the water was too high in the street.

"These people were in real need," says Abungu, " and each of the homeless received a blanket from the government. But when Del Monte said that they had financial problems, they received a thousand acres of land which were taken away from the farmers."

Abungu spits it all out as if I personally have done all this. Or does it just sound like that because I feel guilty since much of this has been done by us, the people from the West? He glances at his watch and asks whether he can do anything for me. He has to go to the classroom and teach his criminals now.

"No, I just called in to say 'hallo.'" If I came in to ask something, I have forgotten it now.

Before he walks to the class he picks up another piece of paper and lets me read it:

> I was hungry and you blamed it on the Communists.
> I was hungry and you circled the moon.
> I was hungry and you told me to wait.
> I was hungry and you set up a commission.
> I was hungry and you said, 'So were my ancestors.'
> I was hungry and you said, 'We don't hire over 35.'
> I was hungry and you said God helps those...
> I was hungry and you told me I shouldn't be.
> I was hungry and you told me machines do that work now.
> I was hungry and you said the poor are always with us.
> Lord, when did we see you hungry?"
>
> (Cf. Matthew 25:37)

This Abungu educates not only the parkingboys...

Love is like a baby, it must be treated tenderly. —Congolese proverb

A FAIRYTALE WEDDING

Kiptoo has a bandage on his foot and his leg is badly swollen. Margaret has a large dressing on her leg too, she has been an invalid for weeks now. They are sitting together outside their poor shacks, in the shadow of the only tree in Kinyago. Actually, it is more of a big bush than a tree, Kiptoo uses it to hang out his washing to dry. It is hard to keep things clean in these dusty slums, but old Kiptoo tries, he does the wash religiously, and the bush is festooned with laundry at the moment.

Kiptoo is reading to Margaret from the newspaper. Yesterday Prince Charles and Diana Spencer were married. The paper is full of it, under the headline 'Fairytale Wedding.' Margaret is fascinated, but she has a question. Why is there nothing in there about Princess Margaret? After all she is family of Prince Charles, and she herself once visited Kenya.

"Why don't you just get yourself baptized again and take the name Diana?" scoffs Kiptoo.

Margaret laughs, and nodding in my direction retorts, "If ever you get to baptize this heathen, you might as well christen him Charles."

"Whatever, our wedding won't be in the paper," Kiptoo assures her.

"I'm not going to marry you, you're not even baptized. *Kiptoo,* what sort of name is that?" Margaret banters.

Kiptoo reckons his name is good enough. He is not so young anymore. I would think he is in his late-sixties—a well-respected man in these parts, with a measure of self-respect too. His plastic-sheeting hut may be tiny, but it is very clean. His bed is not a heap of rags, as with so many. The sheets are folded neatly upon the bare mattress. This harks back to the time when he was with the police force. Order, discipline, neatness, have stuck with him, a leftover from the colonial days.

He was discharged when the war between the whites ended in 1945. No, he did not receive a pension, but there was a letter of recommendation. He made a great deal of use of this in the intervening years, being a nightwatchman in many different places. He is one still, though he is not so good at it anymore. It keeps a wage coming in. He has spent most of his life in Nairobi, and has made an effort to establish himself here. He built himself a house, albeit of sticks and mud, but with a roof as level as a putting-green, and Kiptoo lived here with his wife and three children. Those times ended over fifteen years ago.

1966 was a bad year for Kiptoo. First his wife died, and that was his ruination. A respectable man such as Kiptoo has as much respect for the dead, and he spared no expense for the funeral. That broke him. There was no money left to pay for schooling for the children. And then a couple of months later his house was bulldozed to make room for the new cinema.

That is when Kiptoo came to Kinyago where he set up a rudimentary tent until he could find a place to build his house again. He still lives on the same spot. His children have found their own way; one of his sons lives somewhere in Mathare Valley. "He is a thief," Kiptoo tells me, and he doesn't want anything more to do with him. Here in Kinyago, the man has become poorer and older, and by degrees has lost everything except his *heshima*—his self-respect, his dignity. Kiptoo is leader of the village council, and when I leave the community money with him I know it is in safe hands. What that letter of recommendation says is true: he is honest and dependable.

When Margaret's husband died five years ago, Kiptoo befriended her. He has helped her a great deal, taking more than an interest in bringing up her children. But even with Kiptoo's help, things did not turn out right. Two of the children have undoubtedly taken the wrong path, according to Margaret. Sometime I think that the only way out of Kinyago is via the wrong path. In the last few months we have made an effort to keep the youngest of the children in school, but the outcome is not promising. He is taking the path of so many: the streets.

Margaret was baptized three years ago. Yes, she was baptized before, but that was so long ago that she cannot remember into which church. We spent months in preparation, and Kiptoo often followed along in the discussion and instruction. However, he considered that he had no need to be baptized in order to lead something of a Christian life, just as he had been doing for years.

About a year and a half ago, the entire village of Kinyago had to move—a matter twenty-five meters, in order to make room for a new housing development. Then Kiptoo and Margaret took the opportunity to move their huts next door to one another, by the big bush under which they now sit. During the day, Kiptoo is able to keep an eye on Margaret's possessions whilst she is at work. At night Margaret is there, yet Kiptoo remains at his post. They share their poverty. Kiptoo has the notion that he is going to marry Margaret, but Margaret has no intention of getting married again.

But now they have been together at home for a few days. A little while ago Margaret was bitten by the dog of the European whose garden she looks after three days a week. Even though the European may not discrimate between the races, the dog did. The dog was put down, but that is not a lot of help to Margaret who can still hardly walk. Luckily her wages continue, and on the side she is able to knit many more school uniform sweaters.

Now Kiptoo has a gammy leg too. It looks pretty serious, he can hardly stand on it. When I saw him a couple of days ago he was limping. I asked him what was up, or rather, what was down. I really had a good laugh when he told me, "A duck bit my ankle." Yes, Kiptoo found it very comical too: he, the former policeman, the redoubtable night-watchman, bitten by a duck! But now the leg has become terribly inflamed, and his wages are not going to be paid. On the other hand, this means that he has to take only a minor loss, since he does not earn much in the first place. Margaret makes sure that he has plenty to eat to prevent blood-poisoning, because that can kill you.

As with many of the people here, Kiptoo has a gallows sense of humour, something which is unknown in the countryside. He says, "If you are sick, that is something you can live through, but if you end up dead..." Yes, it is true, if you die you are buried, literally and financially. It kills you and your family too. These people are too poor to die. Margaret wants neither to think about it nor talk about it, and she asks Kiptoo to carry on reading about the fairytale wedding of Charles and Diana. It is not as if Margaret believes in fairytales any more, but that doesn't make them any less beautiful.

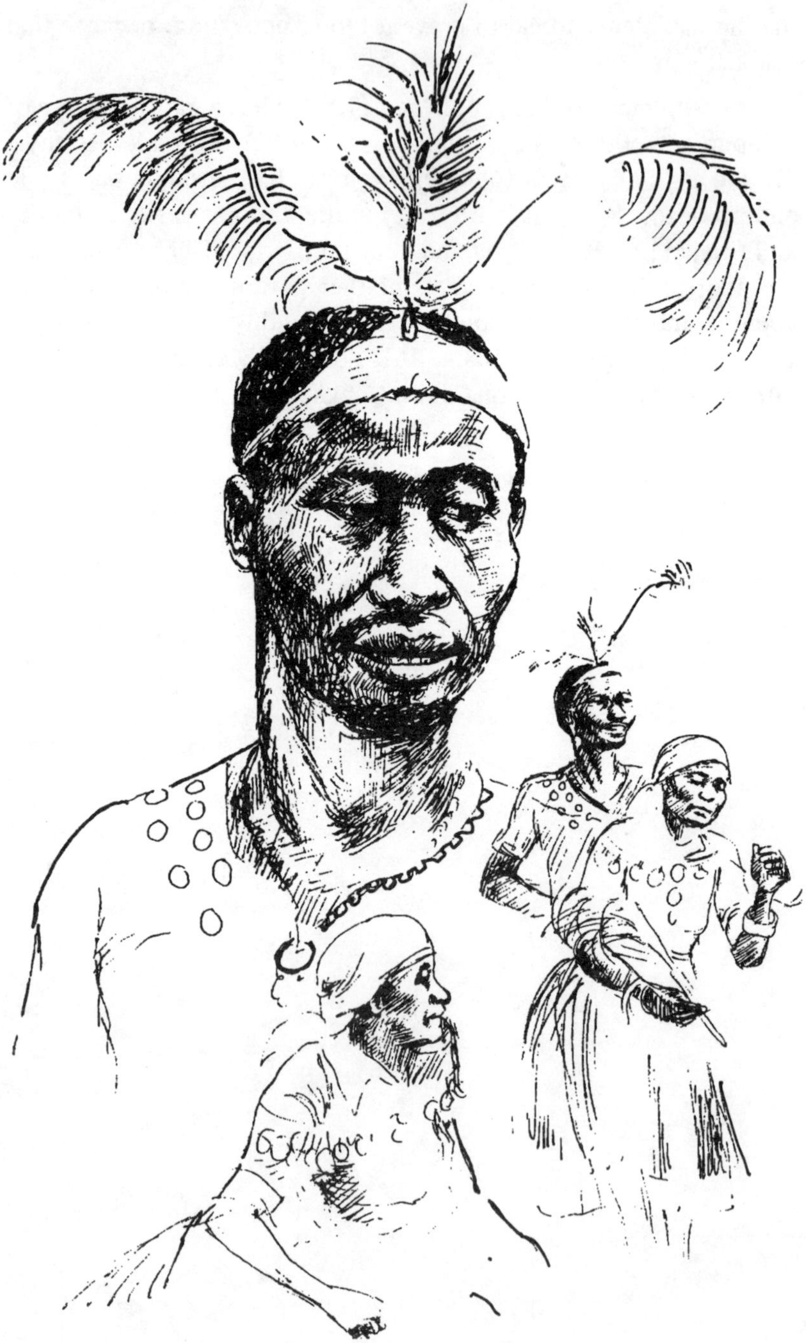

Move your neck according to the music. —ETHIOPIAN SAYING

FULLBLOOD

Even when he's lying on the ground, Mutua can still dance. His whole being moves to the rhythm of the three great drums that accompany the dance troupe. Up he gets, and continues to dance with a girl standing on his shoulders, wiggling her hips. Then he skips in and out of the dancers with a kingly air. He moves his body with a freedom that the others cannot imitate. Together the dancers paint whole stories in their dancing.

Mutua has a special function in the Kamakunji troupe, that of the barker, the attention-getter, like a clown in a circus. Sometimes he will wind up a running jump as if he intends to land in the middle of his public. At the last instant he turns a somersault in mid-air, and then he is standing before me, laughing. He winks and wags his finger as if to say, "You didn't expect that from an old woodcarver did you?" Even while the audience applauds, he is dancing again, this time while walking on his hands.

A couple of months ago, a disco was organized for the young people in his area. Mutua, with all of his forty-five or probably fifty years, was there too. He mixes very well with the youth. That was when he decided it was high time that I, the clumsy priest, should learn to dance. He took me by the hand and led the steps. My dancing was not a success, but the impression Mutua gave, in front of everyone, of the stiff European with two left feet was very well received. That was a good show.

In the morning I went to visit him at his cabin, which also serves as his workplace. I often go to talk with Mutua. For visitors he has provided an old bench seat taken from a Volkswagen van. The upholstery was black in its better years, but I sit in the middle of the chunks of foam rubber and wood shavings that fly around Mutua's hut. He is sitting on the floor on a piece of cardboard, and talks while he busies himself with his woodcarving. He does not actually cut through the block, but with a small, sharp cleaver or hatchet, he gives shape to the piece of wood. His whole abode has the aroma of new wood, other people's places smell of charcoal and sour milk.

I am happy to sit here while Matua talks about his bloodline. That's where he gets his skill from, the dancing too. He has never taken lessons—it is just in the blood.

"You can give it your best shot, but if it isn't in the blood, then nothing will come of it," says he. It is the same with woodcarving. He did not learn that at a trade school. He began to carve at the age of five, his blood is truly that of the Kamba.[15] That is not to say that every Kamba is a woodcarver, but particular clans among them have it in their blood. All they have to do is begin, and they will learn. And Mutua hails from such a clan.

He has worked in various places, in Mombasa, Nakuru, but he has been in Nairobi now for years. His wife, who lives in Kamba-country with their six children, comes looking for him regularly. It is better this way. The city is no place for a child. A woman needs a plot of land for a garden too, according to Mutua. He goes home himself every now and then, to take the school fees, or perhaps if there is the odd cow to be purchased—so long as business is going well.

Mutua is not the best of businessmen. When he has sold all his work, and paid off his debts, he comes to me for a loan to buy new wood. If I say to him that I have the impression paying off his debts is not in his blood, that he still owes me fifty shillings, he replies: "I can carve a good balancing dancer for you, but you'll have to find a coat for me too, because it gets cold in Nairobi in August."

When I went to meet him last Monday, he was looking pretty wretched. I asked if he was sick. No, not sick, he had been celebrating the end of the Moslem fast: *Idd Al Fitr*. Celebrating is in his blood too.

"I thought Moslems didn't drink alcohol," I remarked.

"They can too," said Mutua. "But I'm not a Moslem, I'm a Catholic."

But now he is back to shaping the wood, and by degrees, a dancer appears out of the block.

He talks about his eldest son, who is now working in Nairobi as well, at a job with the city council. Not a woodworker, even though he has Mutua's blood. It looks like the son is earning more than the father, because most woodcarvers are not wealthy. You have to hack and chop plenty to keep five kids in school, but maybe his son can help out now.

As for dancing, that takes up so much time, especially these months when there are so many important visitors. He has to spend the whole day at the airport in order to dance enthusiastically in greeting the visiting heads-of-state and returning ministers. As far a Mutua's concerned, it is a good thing. At heart he is generous.

But those ten shillings he receives for his services, it is too little. Once he complained, but he was hauled off by the cops as a troublemaker. One night in the police station and a fine of fifty shillings. When they let him out he got drunk for two days to celebrate his liberty.

Mutua is a lot like the dancers he carves. They balance on a little pedestal, you can twirl them round and push them from side to side, and they will return to their original position. A full-blooded African indeed.

NOTES

[1] **Undugu:** a Swahili word for brotherhood. Undugu Society of Kenya was started by a missionary, Father Arnold Grol. It started as a youth club, but gradually it has grown into an organization which tries to assist various groups of people in the slums of Nairobi.

[2] **Kikuyu:** The largest tribe in Kenya to which the first President of Kenya, Mzee Jomo Kenyatta, belonged. The Kikuyus are Bantu people.

[3] **Parkingboys:** Usually young boys who try to find parking places for cars. They guard the car and they expect some money for this.

[4] **Chang'aa:** an illegally-distilled gin with a high alcohol content. Often it is badly distilled and poisonous.

[5] **Igloo-village:** the bamboo and plastic huts of the urban poor put one in mind of the snow and ice-dwellings of Eskimos and Aleuts, more than the larger structures of the rural areas in Kenya, on which they are modelled.

[6] **Matatu:** Literally, the word means "three." These taxis used to cost three ten-cent pieces. Now they cost much more, but the nickname 'Threepenny Taxi' remains.

[7] **Sikuma Weeki:** Literally, 'Push the week a bit.' A cheap, green, kale-like vegetable which is eaten with ugali, a maize porridge. It is the vegetable of the poor.

[8] **Jigger:** (Chigger) a larval mite that hatches beneath the skin, causing intense irritation.

[9] **Mau Mau:** the struggle for Kenyan independence from the British, in which many people died during the 1950s and early 60s. Jomo Kenyatta was a leader of the rebellion.

[10] **Mzungu:** Derived from a word which means 'to chase around in circles,' is a term for any white person from Europe, the U.S., Canada, etc. Its use is so general that it bears only faint traces of disrespect, if any. By extension, *Kisungu* is the language of the whites, e.g. English, German, and sometimes legalese.

[11] **Luo:** one of the larger tribal groups in Kenya, traditionally occupying the eastern banks and hinterland of Lake Victoria (Nyanza Province around Kisumu). Luo are considered a Nilotic people.

[12] **Swahili:** A general (and national, though not official) language in Kenya. It has the structure of a Bantu language, but its vocabulary draws from Arabic, and some Portuguese words, as well as a number of coastal languages. Only the coastal Swahili tribe speaks it as a tribal language. Swahili is widespread throughout East Africa and in parts of Central Africa. It is Tanzania's official language.

[13] **Waganga:** Traditional doctors (pl.), their practices and influence vary widely among the traditional cultures. Many incorporate what in the west is known as hypnosis and wholistic medicine in their cures.

[14] **Luya:** a Bantu tribe living mainly in western Kenya.

[15] **Somali:** The Somali tribe are ethnically Hamites. They live in the north of Kenya, bordering Somalia.

[16] **Kamba:** A Bantu tribe, known especially for its woodcarving, traditionally centred on the town of Machakos.

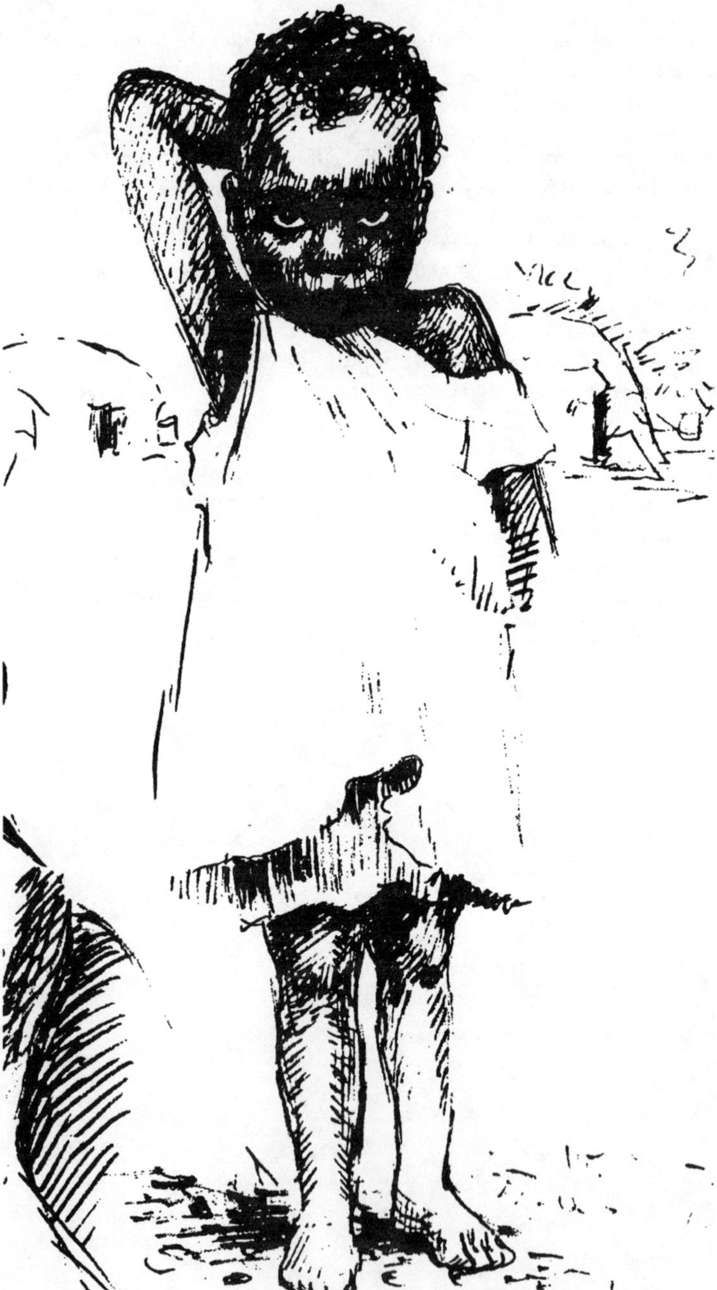